THE WIND CRIES MARY

LOOSELY ADAPTED FROM IBSEN'S *HEDDA GABLER*

BY PHILIP KAN GOTANDA

DRAMATISTS
PLAY SERVICE
INC.

THE WIND CRIES MARY
Copyright © 2004, Philip Kan Gotanda

SPECIAL NOTE

SPECIAL NOTE ON SONGS AND RECORDINGS

The author wishes to thank Diane Takei, Timothy Near, Eric Simonson, Tom Bryant, John McCluggage, Tom Tompkins, Jacqueline Kim, Eric Steinberg, Chay Yew, Diane Matsuda.

AUTHOR'S NOTE

As much as possible I've tried to avoid a sense of parody of the '60s in language and tone. Thus, it's important to downplay styles of the era in costuming and hair.

PREFACE FOR PROGRAM

In the year 1968, there were demonstrations against American involvement in Vietnam taking place on campuses across the country. These demonstrations in turn intersected with the growing unrest of minority students, seeking equal entitlement and representation at college institutions. At campuses like San Francisco State College the young Japanese, Chinese, Filipino and Korean Oriental-American students, inspired by the emergence of Black Movement issues, had renamed themselves Asian-American and had begun to merge their developing identity politics with a broader analysis of the war in Vietnam as part of a global anti-Asian campaign. The Asian-American, African-American and Chicano students at San Francisco State and other institutions were now referring to their united front of minorities as the Third World.

This would be the beginning of a push that would lead to the eventual establishment of Ethnic Studies Departments. Within these there would be a component devoted exclusively to an *Asian-American perspective*. Such a beast had never existed anywhere before. Ever. Segments of the Asian-American populace, especially those in the age range of twenty-five to thirty-five, were caught in the midst of America's changing consciousness of identity, leaving them unsure as to whether they were *Oriental* or *Asian-American*. This play is loosely based on those historical events, as well as events that took place at U.C. Santa Cruz and U.C. Los Angeles as well as at other campuses.

PRE-SHOW LOBBY AND HOUSE MUSIC

The Who, "My Generation" from the *Live at Leeds* album; Kinks, "Well Respected Man"; Rolling Stones, "Spider to the Fly"; Byrds, "Eight Miles High"; Quicksilver, "Messenger Service — Who Do You Love?"; Grateful Dead, "Anthem In the Sun"; Bob Dylan, "Subterranean Homesick Blues"; Paul Butterfield Blues Band, "East West."

CHARACTERS

RAYMOND PEMBERTHY

AUNTIE GLADYS

EIKO HANABI

RACHEL AUWINGER

DR. FRANK NAKADA

MILES KATAYAMA

PLACE AND TIME

San Francisco. 1968.

ACT BREAKDOWN

ACT ONE — morning

ACT TWO — later that afternoon

ACT THREE — early the next morning

ACT FOUR — the following day

THE WIND CRIES MARY was commissioned and originally produced by San Jose Repertory Theatre (Timothy Near, Artistic Director; Alexandra Urbanowski, Managing Director) in San Jose, California, opening on October 25, 2002. It was directed by Eric Simonson; the set and lighting design were by Kent Dorsey; the sound design was by Jeff Mockus; the costume design was by Lydia Tanji; and the stage manager was Bruce Elsperger. The cast was as follows:

RAYMOND PEMBERTHY .... Thomas Vincent Kelly
AUNTIE GLADYS .... Joy Carlin
EIKO HANABI .... Tess Lina
RACHEL AUWINGER .... Allison Sie
DR. FRANK NAKADA .... Sab Shimono
MILES KATAYAMA .... Stan Egi

THE WIND CRIES MARY was written with the support of the California Civil Liberties Public Education Fund, and developed with support from Contemporary Asian Theater Scene and the Fleishhacker Foundation.

" ... somewhere a Queen is weeping ... "

—Jimi Hendrix

" ... the unformed language of articulation for this new world ... the still unshaped face of the new America. We stand so silently. With our breaths held and minds empty, staring out over the abyss. Waiting. Waiting to be filled with the new knowledge ... "

—M. Katayama and E. Hanabi, The Thought Unknown

" ... mental illness as a pathology of liberty ... does no good to treat patient alone ... must treat the cultural and political context also ... "

—Frantz Fanon

" ... I'm a walking, talking, living, loving puppet ... "

— Oldham and Penn song, "I'm Your Puppet"

" ... when you are you, you see things as they are ... "

—D.T. Suzuki

" ... it's a man's world ... "

—James Brown

THE WIND CRIES MARY

ACT ONE

*A song similar to "Not So Sweet Martha Lorraine," the stu-
dio version by Country Joe and the Fish, comes up and plays
for a minute.* Then we gradually begin to bring in news
sound bites reporting American troop activity in Vietnam.
These news reports continue all through the play, giving a con-
tinual sense of growing U.S. involvement, rising death toll
and escalating unrest on college campuses. These reported
activities and events should compress several years into the
course of the play's brief time frame. As lights dim, the music
swells to a high volume, holds, then fades away as the lights
come up. The news is now emanating from the TV at a low
volume.*

*The Pemberthy house. Moving boxes are laid about. A large
stereo console. Color TV is on. Upstage there's an* obutsudan
*(Buddhist shrine) with a photo of Mr. Duke Hanabi promi-
nently displayed next to it. We hear the news about the war in
Vietnam going on in the background. Raymond Pemberthy,
twenty-nine, stands in front of the stereo hi-fi putting a record
on. He wears a kimono loosely thrown over his clothes.
Raymond carefully takes the record out of the jacket, making
sure he doesn't touch the L.P.'s surface. Then he wipes it with
the dust cloth, sets it on the arm and clicks the lever full turn
to make the record drop onto the turntable. It's a song similar
to the We Five's "You were on My Mind."* He stands and listens for a moment, nodding his head. He has no rhythm. He
goes over to the kitchen, bobbing awkwardly to the beat. On
one of the kitchen table's chairs, he notices a moving box
marked "Eiko." He sets it on the table about to look inside,*

* See Special Note on Songs and Recordings on copyright page.

9

then changes his mind. Remembers what he was going to do, goes to the counter and excitedly opens a small, delicately wrapped package containing a canister of tea. Opens it and sprinkles leaves into a teapot. Turns the stove burner on under a pot filled with water. Then he takes out a serving tray preparing to serve tea to Eiko in their bedroom.

Knock at the door. Raymond stops, goes to answer it. It's a mid-fiftyish woman, overweight, dressed in the clothes of an office worker, except with a more stylish, yet unmistakably tacky flair to them. She wears a headband. Holds a large candy box and a folded piece of paper.

RAYMOND. *(Surprised and happy.)* Auntie Gladys, how good to see you!

AUNTIE GLADYS. Welcome home, Raymond ...

RAYMOND. Come in, come —

AUNTIE GLADYS. *(Handing him the box.)* Chocolate bonbons, large size, usually three-fifty a box but I bought three and got a discount so I paid only two ninety-nine for each. Payless. Got stamps, too. And this was on the the porch in front of the door ... *(Hands him the folded note.)* It's from Rachel Auwinger. Apologizing and saying that she came by but realized it was too early and she'll come by later.

RAYMOND. *(Hands now full.)* Oh yes, Rachel Auwinger ...

AUNTIE GLADYS. "You do remember me, don't you, Raymond?" she writes. Of course I remember her, you used to date her. Pretty girl, a bit mousy for my tastes and flat as a pancake. She could be a boy, for all I know. Auntie Vicky — *(Looks sad and shakes her head indicating things don't look good.)* — keeps a stiff upper lip and as long as *General Hospital* stays on the air, she's just dandy. Oh, and she insists we now watch *Bonanza*.

RAYMOND. *(Looking at the note.)* My goodness, hadn't thought of her in a long time, she always smelled so fresh — *(Raymond fixes on her headband.)*

AUNTIE GLADYS. *(Noticing.)* You like? *(She goes straight to the stereo and turns it off without a word, immediately moves to the TV. Shutting it off, referring to the war news.)* They oughta just drop one big bomb on 'em like we did before, that'd solve it. I hope it's not too early, I just had to come by and see how you were. You look tired, dear, you been getting enough rest?

RAYMOND. I'm fine, all the traveling, that's all.

AUNTIE GLADYS. The bride?

RAYMOND. Eiko's still sleeping, I was going to bring her some special tea.

AUNTIE GLADYS. Still in bed, at this hour? My goodness, she *is* a princess ...

RAYMOND. Jet lag, you know ...

AUNTIE GLADYS. *(Looking around.)* Jeez Louise, they just left everything all over. I told the movers which rooms to put the boxes in. I put away most things but what I wasn't sure about I left in their boxes, I know how particular she is. I didn't know you read *Playboy* magazine? Well, you don't need to look at those sluts anymore when you got the real thing, huh?

RAYMOND. What's with the — *(Motioning to her head.)*

AUNTIE GLADYS. What do you think, all the kids on campus are wearing them now and well, I know how stylish Eiko is and I wanted to, you know, let her know your auntie has some style in her, too ...

RAYMOND. Ahh, you don't have to worry about that Auntie, you're always stylish in my eyes. *(Auntie Gladys goes over and smooches Raymond.)*

AUNTIE GLADYS. Oh, you're too sweet to me — aren't you going to open it?

RAYMOND. What? Oh, okay.

AUNTIE GLADYS. These are special, have nuts inside along with the nougat. *(Looking around at the house, impressed.)* My ...

RAYMOND. You know, we wanted to both thank you for helping with the move, Eiko was in such a hurry to leave on the honeymoon ...

AUNTIE GLADYS. She gets a bee in her bonnet, it seems nothing can stop her no matter who has to pick up after her. Comes from being an only child and spoiled by her rich daddy. I'm glad you weren't raised that way. *(Auntie Gladys walks around the house, opening the curtains.)*

RAYMOND. Japan was quite illuminating, the gender roles are fascinating. On the surface, yes, it appears the woman is subservient to the man, which I might say — off the record, of course, lest the libbies bite my head off — was a refreshing thought compared to American male-female dynamic. But in fact a simple system of division of labor has been developed such that the woman alone raises the child — the father, the salaryman, absent, being forced to work all day and then drink till all hours — and is, the woman that is, in the end the true steward and progenitor of cultural mores. And — this is interesting — thus the unsung motor of its fledgling economic boom, the child taking on an overdeveloped sense of dependency on the mother, and in turn, as an adult, transferring this filial allegiance on to the *zaibatsu*, or big corporations, which become the new surrogate mother-parent — known to house, feed and at times even arrange marriages for their children as it were — guaranteeing the continuum of social and economic order, the zeitgeist of Japan, an eerie hybrid of family values and filial allegiance to the company god. One could argue it's a woman's world. *(Auntie Gladys has ended up in front of the photo by the shrine.)*

AUNTIE GLADYS. This him?

RAYMOND. Her father, the one and only, Duke Hanabi.

AUNTIE GLADYS. *(Shaking her head.)* Looks like he just got off the boat.

RAYMOND. The shrine was the first thing Eiko wanted unpacked. *(Beat.)* Oh, and especially thank you for helping out with the, you know …

AUNTIE GLADYS. Oh, you never mind, anything for my little Raymond and his new bride.

RAYMOND. I finally told Eiko about Dr. Nakada helping us.

AUNTIE GLADYS. He did all the work. I didn't have to do anything. *(Looking around.)* It is a bit overwhelming, though. I never woulda imagined you living in a place quite like this …

RAYMOND. Nice?

AUNTIE GLADYS. Large.

RAYMOND. You like it?

AUNTIE GLADYS. Very big.

RAYMOND. She saw it and fell in love with it. So I did, too. *(Raymond has brought over the box of candies and holds it to allow Auntie Gladys to take another bonbon, but she takes the whole box. Raymond smiles and goes back to the kitchen to pour the hot water into the teapot.)*

AUNTIE GLADYS. To tell you the truth, I'm still amazed she married you. Nothing against you Raymond but it's not like she didn't have the pick of the litter. Auntie Vicky— *(Looks sad and shakes her head, then right back to the conversation.)* — and I talked about this. I mean, her type usually don't go for someone with your paycheck, they usually like one of those country club types …

RAYMOND. *(Taking the tea tray up the stairs to the bedroom.)* Not once I get the teaching position and Dr. Nakada said it's in the bag — He's really been so helpful ...

AUNTIE GLADYS. *(Not noticing he's left, eating bonbons all through this speech.)* Only Oriental. You know they do have 'em in Hawaii I read. Oriental Rockefellers. Her father was one, not in Hawaii, here I mean. The girls in the office heard stories about him, he was quite the character. Heard he liked the Mamie Van Doren type, if you know what I mean, and what the hello does she see in that baseball player, what's his name ... Dr. Nakada knew him, the father, guess they did some business together. He said he lost everything cause when he drank it made him stupid. Bo Belinsky! But while she was growing up? Like a little Oriental princess. Such a short courtship, too. I can tell you now we did wonder if there was a bun in the oven, if you know what I mean — *(Raymond reappears coming down the stairs after dropping off the tea.)*

RAYMOND. What's that about the oven?

AUNTIE GLADYS. *(Without missing a beat.)* — No thanks, I have to watch my figure — which, well, still woulda surprised us, me in particular cause, well, you never really dated girls that much and these things take a little know-how and you never really showed much of any know-how in those areas. 'Course maybe we're to blame, me and your Auntie Vicky — *(Shakes her head sadly.)* — 'cause we're just not good talking about those things — your father, our brother — he would've been good at it, too good at it actually. But maybe it's okay because, well, let's face it, she *is* more sophisticated than you, if you know what I mean. *(Eiko appears on the stairs, unseen by Raymond or Auntie Gladys, and observes. Raymond busies himself in the kitchen area.)* There are those rumors, especially about getting kicked out of college, you know, the boy in the dorm room thing? And a particularly disgusting rumor the boy was colored. But still we were all surprised when you two got together seeing as who she is and seeing as who you are. But then it's not like you don't have anything to offer 'cause after all you're, I mean, let's be honest, you're Caucasian and she's not and I think it balances things out, you know. Then there's — me and Auntie Vicky *(Shakes her head.)* talked about this — the baby — which we hope to hear some news about soon — to think about, being half-Oriental and all. *(Eiko withdraws up the stairs.)* Still, we want to support you and you come saying you need to have this house so what should you do, so I ask around the office and Dr. Nakada, who's pretty high up in the business school and sort of my boss 'cause I do work in that department's office, he offers to handle it and since he knew her father and well …

RAYMOND. Would you like some tea, also?

AUNTIE GLADYS. I used my own money on the down.

RAYMOND. What?

AUNTIE GLADYS. My nest egg. For your house.

RAYMOND. I thought Dr. Nakada was arranging a loan through folks he knew.

AUNTIE GLADYS. Yes, but it wasn't enough and there was also the size of those monthly mortgage payments, we both thought it just might be too big …

RAYMOND. Your savings, Auntie?

AUNTIE GLADYS. Yes.

RAYMOND. But that's all you have. You're living off it.

AUNTIE GLADYS. You're my brother's son, I couldn't do less. And who knows, maybe if I need to, if things work out that way, you know with Auntie Vicky — *(She shakes her head very sadly.)* — I could, you know, if I got lonely and needed a place to stay …

RAYMOND. *(Understanding.)* Oh, yes, yes, of course, wouldn't that be so nice …

AUNTIE GLADYS. *(Getting excited.)* Especially when we start to hear the pitter-patter of little feet, you're going to need some help.

RAYMOND. Oh, Auntie, I do love you, but I worry, that was all you had.

AUNTIE GLADYS. Dr. Nakada said it wouldn't be a problem, what with you getting the teaching position, a large raise in salary, and I heard that Eiko was quite the chemistry whiz, I'm sure she can get a job at the college — *(Eiko Hanabi enters down the stairs. Twenty-nine, striking, carries herself with a sense of breeding and class.)*

EIKO. Who's getting a job?

RAYMOND. Oh, you're up. I thought you'd stay in bed for a bit longer.

EIKO. I don't drink barley tea. Hello Gladys, what brings you over so early? Make some coffee for all of us, Raymond.

RAYMOND. But we're having … *(Eiko has walked past the box of candies, directly over to the curtains that Auntie Gladys has opened and proceeds to close them.)*

AUNTIE GLADYS. My, but you're looking stunning as always. Did you get the dress over there?

RAYMOND. Auntie couldn't wait to see us and say hello. Find out how our trip was.

14

EIKO. I got this in New York last season, Saks. It was awful, the Orient, I hated it.

RAYMOND. *(Keeping the conversation light.)* We stayed up all night watching *The Invisible Man* — Claude Raines, I always get him mixed up with Adolph Monjou ...

EIKO. Funny, the *man*, you could see him even when he was invisible ... *(Noticing and picking it up.)* Oh, look, one of the movers left these cheap candies.

RAYMOND. Eiko.

EIKO. Hmm?

AUNTIE GLADYS. They aren't cheap. I bought them on sale but they aren't cheap.

RAYMOND. Auntie brought them, they're really very good.

AUNTIE GLADYS. Just because it's Payless, doesn't mean they're cheap.

EIKO. Oh, I'm sorry. I don't eat these types of candies so I don't know.

AUNTIE GLADYS. Some of us happen to know the value of a dollar. I know Raymond does.

RAYMOND. Try one. Please?

EIKO. Of course, maybe later. *(To Auntie Gladys.)* I am sorry ... *(Eiko spots the storage box with her name sitting on the kitchen table.)* I need my coffee first. *(Eiko quickly crosses over and sets the box inside the back room and closes the French doors.)*

RAYMOND. Auntie, you were having tea, weren't you? Or did you want coffee?

AUNTIE GLADYS. Sure, sure, whatever we're having, dear. What are we having?

RAYMOND. Eiko, I thought you'd like the tea. Remember, we bought it from that nice little farmer near your father's village. *(Eiko moving to the counter.)*

EIKO. *You* bought it.

RAYMOND. *(To Auntie Gladys.)* It's called *mugi cha*, made from barley.

AUNTIE GLADYS. *(Impressed.)* Oh, my, that sounds exotic. I guess I'm one of the family, now.

RAYMOND. Come on, Eiko.

EIKO. *(Getting out instant coffee for herself.)* That's why my father left there, so his daughter wouldn't have to drink *peasant's* tea. *(Auntie Gladys stares at her tea and puts it down.)*

RAYMOND. Everybody drinks it now. Especially during the

summers, chilled. Honey, I'll make your coffee ... *(Raymond leading Eiko over to the sofa.)* Go, go, sit down and visit with Auntie, I'll make it for you. *(Eiko and Auntie Gladys sit down across from each other. Awkward silence.)*

AUNTIE GLADYS. So we have a doctor in the house now.

EIKO. Excuse me?

RAYMOND. She means me, now that I have my doctorate.

EIKO. Oh, that kind of doctor. I thought you meant a real doctor.

AUNTIE GLADYS. You're still called a doctor, aren't you? They call you doctor, right?

RAYMOND. Well, yes, of course.

EIKO. I just meant not like a medical doctor, that's all.

AUNTIE GLADYS. A doctor's a doctor, my nephew's a doctor.

RAYMOND. I'm a doctor, Auntie.

AUNTIE GLADYS. I know you're a doctor.

EIKO. Just not a medical doctor. *(Pause. Auntie Gladys holds out the box of candy to Eiko who pretends not to see it, casually looking away. Auntie Gladys doesn't move it. It sits out there. Eiko will have nothing to do with it. Auntie Gladys gets up and stands beside Eiko, holding the candy in front of her nose. Finally, Eiko takes one and stares at it.)*

AUNTIE GLADYS. Yes, yes, come on now, you can do it ...

RAYMOND. Auntie, maybe you shouldn't ...

EIKO. That's all right, Raymond. *(Eiko takes a very small bite.)*

AUNTIE GLADYS. Over the lips and through the gums, look out stomach, here it comes ...

EIKO. *(To Raymond.)* You had an interesting childhood, I take it.

AUNTIE GLADYS. *(Making an announcement, with emphasis to Eiko.)* We watch *Bonanza* now! *(Eiko and Raymond stare at her. Moving back to her seat.)* Oh, I heard some news about that dreadful friend of yours, ex-friend of yours, what's his name, the one that went nuts and they had to kick him off the faculty ...

RAYMOND. You mean Miles Katayama?

AUNTIE GLADYS. Un-huh, that one. They were talking about him in the president's office. He wrote some new book or something. Elsie in the office told me, they have a copy over at the sociology department.

EIKO. Miles Katayama?

AUNTIE GLADYS. *(Nodding.)* Un-huh.

RAYMOND. He has a book out? Really? I find that hard to believe.

AUNTIE GLADYS. I saw the book jacket, you should see his

photo. He looked as silly as ever — hair in a ponytail, and that Chinaman's moustache — what do they call it …

RAYMOND. Auntie, you don't say, "Chinaman."

EIKO. I think it's more correct to say, "Chink."

RAYMOND. I didn't know he was writing again.

AUNTIE GLADYS. Then what do you call someone from China — "Hey, you!"? *(Muttering.)* Besides, we watch *Bonanza* now …

RAYMOND. *(To Eiko.)* You know Miles, don't you?

EIKO. A little, from the old days.

AUNTIE GLADYS. Terrible fellow — drugs, student strikes, getting arrested — he hit a policeman, you know that. *(Brings coffee over for Eiko.)*

RAYMOND. He didn't hit a policeman, he resisted arrest.

AUNTIE GLADYS. Oh, like they're different … *(Raymond, Auntie sit in silence, munching on candies. Eiko sips her coffee, lost in thought.)* Fu Manchu! *(Auntie Gladys giggles self-consciously. They return to munching on chocolates. Noticing, to Eiko:)* You got a little fat.

EIKO. Excuse me?

RAYMOND. She filled out a bit, huh. More of her to hold onto now.

AUNTIE GLADYS. More in the face, the cheeks. Like a chipmunk.

EIKO. I don't think so …

RAYMOND. *(Noticing.)* You are getting a little tummy …

EIKO. I am not.

AUNTIE GLADYS. *(Wondering.)* Oh, really?

EIKO. *(Getting up and moving to the counter.)* You always make my coffee too weak — it's the style of the cut, the material drapes funny and can give that impression …

AUNTIE GLADYS. *(Cheering up.)* Oh, well, yes, of course.

EIKO. I'm not gaining weight.

RAYMOND. I don't mind, I always thought you were kinda skinny.

AUNTIE GLADYS. *(Announcing.)* And besides your book is going to be a much bigger hit than that Communist agitator, Mr. "Hey, you!" *(Getting up, suddenly with renewed vigor.)* Well, I better be getting back to the office. I'm going to stop by and see Auntie Vicky first. The girls are covering for me and I'm already late. We're trying to get our work done before the demonstration starts.

RAYMOND. You be careful.

AUNTIE GLADYS. And who knows how long we could get stuck in the building — police, tear gas, my goodness. And you deary, you should get as much rest as you can. Well, you know what I mean …

17

EIKO. No, I don't know what you mean.

RAYMOND. You have to leave already?

AUNTIE GLADYS. *(Touching her headband, in Eiko's direction.)* All the kids are wearing them on campus, especially the ones who take drugs.

RAYMOND. *(Playfully scolding.)* Auntie, you hippie …

AUNTIE GLADYS. *(To Eiko.)* You should get one. *(To Raymond.)* I'm sure you two want to be alone. Make sure she gets plenty of rest and drinks lots of milk. *(Raymond escorts Auntie Gladys to the door and sees her out. Eiko is upset and mad. She takes the box of chocolates and stuffs it into the garbage, using her foot to bash it down violently. Raymond enters and heads over to the stereo. Eiko moves to the counter to add more instant coffee to her cup.)*

RAYMOND. What was Auntie talking about, rambling on and on like that?

EIKO. Four spoonfuls, I've told you before, I like it strong … *(Raymond puts on a band like We Five again.* Starts to dance, very badly towards Eiko.)*

RAYMOND. See, the thing about the We Five is it's the bridge to today's music. Being an old folkie, it allows me to understand the music the kids are listening to these days. *(Dancing, sort of.)* See, I know how to be groovy. *(Trying to get Eiko to dance.)* "Kimono my house, I'll show you my koto" … *(Eiko ignores him and goes to the stereo and turns up the volume. Stands next to it, sipping her coffee and listening. Raymond wonders what's going on. Yelling over:)* What are you doing?

EIKO. This is killing me!

RAYMOND. *(Shouting.)* What?

EIKO. It's killing me!

RAYMOND. What?

EIKO. It's killing — *(Raymond lifts the needle off the record.)* … me.

RAYMOND. What's killing you?

EIKO. It's too early to be playing that kind of music.

RAYMOND. It's never too early to play rock 'n' roll.

EIKO. The We Five is not rock and roll.

RAYMOND. Yes, it is. I got it from one of my students, he has hair down to his shoulders.

EIKO. Jimi Hendrix is rock and roll.

RAYMOND. Negro people do not play rock 'n' roll. He's an anomaly. Even the Motown folks won't claim him as one of theirs.

---

* See Special Note on Songs and Recordings on copyright page.

I read in *Rolling Stone* his stepmother is Japanese, up in Seattle. I wonder what nationality Ben Fong-Torres is? How come you know about Jimi Hendrix?

EIKO. Just because I don't like that kind of music doesn't mean I don't *know* about that kind of music.

RAYMOND. And that's what I love. I never know what you're going to surprise me with next. There's only one thing.

EIKO. What?

RAYMOND. If you could call Auntie Gladys, *Auntie* Gladys.

EIKO. Why? She's not my aunt.

RAYMOND. Yes, but I know it'd make her so happy to hear you say it.

EIKO. Her happiness was your concern. *My* happiness is your concern now. You're married to me, aren't you?

RAYMOND. Yes, I know that, honey, but — okay, all right. What would you like to hear … *(Raymond goes to the stereo and looks through the albums.)*

EIKO. *(Refering to the coffee she's sipping.)* Ahhh, that's more like it. The first cup you made was like water. I like coffee that bites back, let's you know it's there. Four spoonfuls, four spoonfuls. *(Raymond puts on a song similar to Erik Satie's "Trois Gymnopedie."*)*

RAYMOND. How's that? Better?

EIKO. Don't ever take me to Japan again. I hate the toilets, I hate the baths, I hate the food, I especially hate anything raw, I hate the crowdedness, I hate how everything is so small, I hate that they can't speak English, I hate even more that they can't *understand* English. I hate the way the women all cater to the men. And I hate how they all stare at me like I'm some kind of freak because I look like I'm Japanese but I act American and there's a very good reason for it because I *am* American, goddamnit!

RAYMOND. Okay …

EIKO. There's one thing I want you to know.

RAYMOND. Yes, honey?

EIKO. I'd rather kill myself than get fat. *(Raymond's not sure how to take this. Turns off the stereo and changes the topic.)*

RAYMOND. *(Referring to the house.)* What do you think of it? Is it what you thought it would be? I'm a little overwhelmed to tell you the truth.

EIKO. I wished to God you hadn't used Nakada to get the loan. What am I supposed to do here all day long?

* See Special Note on Songs and Recordings on copyright page.

RAYMOND. *(Under his breath.)* Hopefully not get fat.

EIKO. What?

RAYMOND. Hopefully get unpacked. Auntie Gladys said he offered to help — was only too happy to help. *(Eiko walks around looking at the place. She goes through the French doors into the back and hits a single note on the piano four times. She holds the sustain and it lingers.)*

EIKO. *(Offstage.)* If I'm going to use this one for now, it needs to be tuned. *(Note lingering in the air for a long moment. Doorbell rings. Raymond goes to answer it. Eiko releases the note and reenters the room, going to the* obutsudan. *Touches her father's picture. Raymond enters with Rachel Auwinger, twenty-seven, very pretty in a girlish fashion, though now with a bust. Nervous, a bit high-strung. She carries a knapsack. She looks slightly hippie-esque, but not overdone.)*

RACHEL. I was worried you wouldn't remember me.

RAYMOND. This is a surprise. *(To Eiko.)* This is Rachel Auwinger, an old friend of mine. *(Leaning in.)* Is it still Auwinger?

RACHEL. Cohen, now.

RAYMOND. *(Announcing.)* Cohen now, Rachel Cohen.

RACHEL. Hello Miss Hanabi. I apologize for coming over unannounced, I came by earlier but I realized you were probably still sleeping so I left a note under the door — I signed it Auwinger so if you did remember me, you'd remember me — and walked around the neighborhood till now. *(Raymond pulls the note out of his pocket and waves it around self-consciously.)*

RAYMOND. Yes, we got it. *(Leaning in to Rachel.)* It's Mrs. Pemberthy now.

RACHEL. Oh, yes, I heard, that's right, that's right, I'm sorry, Mrs. Pemberthy. I'm so used to thinking of you as Eiko Hanabi, that's how everyone knew you. You probably don't remember me — I was two years behind you at Japanese language school.

EIKO. I didn't attend very long.

RACHEL. You used to make me eat dirt.

RAYMOND. Sit, sit. What exactly did you want to see us about?

RACHEL. *(Sincere.)* It's good to see you again Raymond. The years have been good to you.

RAYMOND. Yes, well … I almost didn't recognize you, you've … You look great … *(Awkward beat. He looks back at Eiko.)*

RACHEL. I live up north now. Just outside of Portland, Oregon? I didn't mean to come to you folks but he mentioned he used to know you *(To Eiko.)* and since I didn't know who to turn to I looked up *(To Raymond.)* your name under information and got your address and came over here. It was under new listings. *(Raymond and Eiko are not sure who she's referring to. Realizing:)* Oh, you don't know who I'm talking about, I'm sorry, yes, it's Miles Katayama, you know him right? I just know he's going to get into trouble, I know it, so I had to come down here and find him.

EIKO. Miles Katayama?

RACHEL. Yes, you do know him, don't you?

RAYMOND. We both know him. I taught an undergraduate course with him at San Jose State.

EIKO. What's he doing in town?

RACHEL. Oh, he shouldn't have left our place. He thinks he's fine, he's ready now that his book is about to come out. But he's really not ready yet.

RAYMOND. Ready to what?

EIKO. How do you know Miles?

RACHEL. Oh — I'm sorry, yes, I haven't explained everything, I live outside Portland — oh, I said that already — anyway, my husband teaches at Reed College, Lawrence Cohen, you may have heard his name, he's kinda controversial — been experimenting with some of Ronald Laing's theories, radical psychiatry?

RAYMOND. I think so …

EIKO. R.D., he's a Brit.

RACHEL. Actually it's a commune. We live there with five other families from the college — all from the Psych Department, mainly Abnormal. I met Miles at the commune, he's an acquaintance of one of the wives, or girlfriends, they're not really married but they have a baby — not Miles but his acquaintance's boyfriend or husband — we think it's his baby, or maybe my husband's, oh Jesus, that's a whole other story — anyway, he needed a place to stay.

EIKO. Miles?

RACHEL. Yes. He was a wreck. He was underground for a while because of his anti-war activities. Quite frankly, he was hard to understand, almost incoherent. Burned out, totally. But we all could tell he was different so we let him stay. He tutored the kids to pay for his keep. He's really quite brilliant. I realized that the moment I met him. So did my husband. I was trying to help him get back on his feet, stay healthy, start writing again, but Larry convinced him to —

RAYMOND. Your husband?

RACHEL. Yes, my husband, Lawrence, I call him Larry — he

21

convinced Miles to take part in his research, a new experimental "blow out" treatment he's been developing with several others in the commune involving cohabitating for periods of time with schizophrenics who have been purposely taken off Thorazine so they're in full-blown schizophrenic happy hour —

EIKO. *(Impatient to move the story along.)* The idea is to create a climate for the patient to have a guided benign and healthy mental breakdown. You're supposed to come out at the other end — if you come out — with a whole newly integrated consciousness about the world ...

RAYMOND. Where did you learn —

RACHEL. Yes, and Miles? Thrust into this room of full-bloom psychoses? I mean he wanted to do it, volunteered — and it worked, scrambled his brain in a good way, but I nearly lost him, too. His mind is still fragile but then the last six months, he's been amazingly prolific. We were getting so much good work done.

EIKO. You say he's in town now?

RACHEL. What? Yes.

EIKO. Do you know where he is?

RACHEL. Yes, I found out where he's staying.

EIKO. Well, why don't we invite him over? And you can be here, also.

RACHEL. Oh, yes, that would be good.

RAYMOND. Why don't you just go over there and see him yourself? *(Pause.)*

RACHEL. I don't think I could do that ...

EIKO. She can't do that.

RAYMOND. Why not? *(Eiko observes Rachel as she addresses her.)*
EIKO. That's why you came over here, isn't it? *(Rachel is silent.)* You don't know a thing about women, Raymond.

RAYMOND. I thought that's what all this bra burning was about? So a woman doesn't have to be all quiet and demure, she can grab the club and go after the man herself?

EIKO. Bra burning doesn't accomplish anything. The men get more to ogle and the breasts just sag sooner. Now if you got rid of the breasts ... Where's he staying?

RACHEL. At the York Hotel.

EIKO. Raymond, call over there and invite him over tonight. *(To Rachel.)* How's that?

RACHEL. That'd be wonderful. Oh, I knew you could help.

RAYMOND. Now?

EIKO. Now.

RAYMOND. Tonight?

EIKO. Tonight.

RAYMOND. *(Leaving to the back room.)* Okay …

EIKO. *(Scooting him along.)* Yes, go, go … *(Once Raymond has left, Eiko pulls Rachel over and makes her sit next to her on the couch.)* Come over here Rachel. Come on. I do remember you from Japanese school.

RACHEL. I got the feeling you didn't.

EIKO. I do now. I mean how many *happa* kids were there in the classes?

RACHEL. That's true.

EIKO. And I didn't make you eat dirt.

RACHEL. Yes, yes, you did 'cause I was half-white — you all teased me. I haven't forgotten.

EIKO. No, I liked you Rachel.

RACHEL. Funny way of showing it.

EIKO. Really, I did.

RACHEL. Truth is I hated you.

EIKO. Oh.

RACHEL. Those were very confusing times for me. Didn't know if I wanted to be Japanese or Caucasian. Trouble was neither one wanted me. *(Eiko studies Rachel who's uncomfortable under her gaze.)*

EIKO. Does your husband know you're down here?

RACHEL. Of course.

EIKO. He doesn't, does he?

RACHEL. Why would you say a thing like that?

EIKO. And you've been working with Miles? *Closely? (Awkward beat.)*

RACHEL. He says I'm his muse —

EIKO. *(Interrupts.)* His muse?

RACHEL. Un-huh, I've gotten him to trust himself again. To trust the world. He doesn't drink, smoke dope, take any chemicals anymore. He told me he'd be dead if it weren't for me.

EIKO. I see …

RACHEL. I just have to see him, make sure he's okay. He told me about some woman who nearly drove him mad. She's here. I worry he'll get mixed up with her again.

EIKO. Did he say who this person was?

RACHEL. I think it's a singer with one of the bands he used to hang out with. Do you know which one? He said she almost killed him.

EIKO. What else did he say?

RACHEL. That maybe that's what he wanted. That's why I'm so worried. *(Beat.)* Mary. I think that's what he called her. Mary.

EIKO. Mary … *(Eiko is quiet for moment. Then turns her attention back to Rachel.)* Those were difficult times for me, too — our time together in Japanese School. I bet you didn't know that I was born in Japan. Yamanashi area. My mother died when I was quite young and then after the War we came to the States —

RACHEL. I'm sorry about your mother, I didn't know.

EIKO. No, no, she would run after him like a skitterish mouse, waiting on him hand and foot, quite pitiful actually. Anyway, the point is I was secretly an FOB. When I made fun of others I was really making fun of me. You hated me? I hated me more. *(Eiko watches her for a beat, then gets up.)* I believe the band you're referring to might be Mad River — I read they're playing at the Fillmore, this weekend. I think Miles used to run into them at those anti-war benefits he was speaking at. They have a female singer that Miles knows.

RACHEL. I thought so. We have to help him. His work is getting so good but his state is delicate still, he can be a little paranoid. You should read his new paper. He's quite mad, he's doing it all long-hand, page after page, like it's being dictated to him from some mysterious place. He's drawing from so many sources — " … the apocalypse is here right now. The children, the insane and deformed of soul can see it as they live outside the boundaries of institutionalized consciousness. The worm needs to die first, all of it, and we must help it." He's got it all in his knapsack. I have all his notes in here — *(Raymond enters.)*

RAYMOND. I left a message at the front desk. At least we know he's there.

RACHEL. When he comes over, maybe he can read some of it, his new paper? So you can hear what we've been doing?

RAYMOND. You mean the book?

EIKO. No, this is more recent, new stuff.

RAYMOND. Oh, I don't think he'd want anyone to hear his ideas before he's published them.

EIKO. Nonsense, we're all friends — you think he would? Ms. Muse to Miles?

RACHEL. Oh, he wouldn't mind, besides the ideas are so visionary most folks wouldn't know what to think anyway. "We must help the worm die — "

EIKO. *(Interrupts.)* Something along the lines of, "so the butterfly can be born." Mr. Katayama's very eclectic, isn't he — drawing from Alejandro Jodorowsky, Chilean filmmaker. Jodorowsky's command of English is limited so he mixes up worm for caterpiller — " ... you and I will be the first movements in the wings of the great butterfly." *(Awkward pause.)* Well, there. We're all set.

RACHEL. Yes, this is wonderful. It might help him to stay on track. You could help him, Raymond. You seem much more politic than he is. He doesn't know how to play the academic game. You've got such a sensible head on your shoulders. He seems to offend people on purpose some times.

RAYMOND. Well, let's see what happens tonight. It's been a while since I've seen him.

EIKO. Yes, now you must go and rest, you look very weary.

RACHEL. I am. *(Beat.)* It's really good to see you, Raymond.

RAYMOND. And I, you. *(Doorbell rings. Exiting:)* Jeez, what's going on — I'll get it.

EIKO. Where are you staying?

RACHEL. I'm crashing at the faculty guest housing. *(Eiko leads Rachel out as we hear Raymond letting Dr. Nakada in. We hear them meeting in the hallway OS. Raymond and Dr. Nakada entering. Fiftyish, good shape, thinks of himself as a ladies' man. A moustache, sideburns and slightly long hair are his acknowledgement to the changing styles.)*

RAYMOND. I wanted to thank you for helping out with the, you know ...

DR. NAKADA. Yes, umm, nice-looking girl — she's half-Oriental?

RAYMOND. *(Nodding.)* Un-huh, half-Caucasian.

DR. NAKADA. What's her name again?

RAYMOND. Married to a Professor Lawrence Cohen, up at Reed College. Rachel, used to be Rachel Auwinger, she's from around here, Eiko knows her.

DR. NAKADA. Lawrence Cohen ... Ahh that one, the hippie psychiatrist, got arrested a few years back — something about cavorting around with young, naked girls — caused quite a stir. *(Looking towards the door.)* For such an old geezer, he's doing all right ... *(Beat.)* I'm actually glad I have you alone for a moment.

RAYMOND. What, is there a problem? The loan? Auntie said you thought there was nothing to worry about.

DR. NAKADA. Well, yes and no.

RAYMOND. Yes and no?

DR. NAKADA. First off, as your informal financial advisor, you've bitten off quite a bit, what with the house and now this extended trip through Asia.

RAYMOND. It was our honeymoon.

DR. NAKADA. Yes, but given the monies you put into this place, I don't think it was all that prudent to compound your debt with such an extravagant trip.

RAYMOND. Eiko was so excited about traveling —

DR. NAKADA. I know how Eiko can be, you don't have to tell me, I knew the old man only too well. Now there's something else too.

RAYMOND. The "no" part?

DR. NAKADA. Did you know that Miles Katayama was back at the college?

RAYMOND. Yes, as a matter of fact.

DR. NAKADA. And that he has a book coming out, I believe with a major mainstream press? *(Eiko enters.)*

RAYMOND. Not an academic press ...

EIKO. Rachel mentioned it, the book part.

RAYMOND. That's probably why we didn't hear about it.

EIKO. As well as Raymond's aunt.

DR. NAKADA. Well it's getting a lot of attention. He sent advance copies all around and it's causing quite a stir. He's definitely gotten his act together — not only does he write but he knows how to promote, too.

EIKO. I'm sure it was Rachel who did it.

DR. NAKADA. The girl who just left?

RAYMOND. She's a friend of his, she's been helping him write.

EIKO. This is up at Reed College. His muse ...

DR. NAKADA. That's where he's been ...

RAYMOND. So what's the problem?

DR. NAKADA. The teaching position.

RAYMOND. The teaching position? You said it was a done deal, there was no other real competition ... *(Pause. Realizing.)* Miles, that's why he's in town ... *(Nakada nods.)*

EIKO. He's applying for the same position?

DR. NAKADA. Apparently so.

RAYMOND. So he's going to get it?

DR. NAKADA. No, it doesn't mean he's going to get it but it's not a shoo-in for you anymore.

EIKO. Oh my. A competition.

RAYMOND. What? This isn't a game Eiko, we need for me to get the position.

DR. NAKADA. Well. I just wanted to let you folks know the situation so you can better plan in regards to any future expenditures. May I suggest you two have a meeting about this, get a handle on it. I better be going.

RAYMOND. I'll see you out.

EIKO. Dr. Nakada? *(Nakada stops.)* I understand we have you to thank for the loan on the house. *(Beat.)*

DR. NAKADA. Yes, yes you do. *(Beat.)* I do hope we'll be seeing you at the club now that you're back. Your father always cut a colorful figure there. I do say, we all could use another Hanabi there again.

RAYMOND. Pemberthy.

DR. NAKADA. Yes, well … *(Raymond exits with Dr. Nakada. Eiko seems oddly giddy. Raymond returns, distraught.)*

RAYMOND. This is not good. You don't think they'll really give the position to Miles? I mean, after all the trouble he's caused with his speeches and organizing and the way he left the college?

EIKO. *(Musing.)* Raymond and Miles going for the same position.

RAYMOND. Eiko? I need this position so we can meet all our obligations.

EIKO. A little competitive spirit never hurt anyone. Suddenly, I feel as if my life is full again. As if there's a reason to get up now.

RAYMOND. I'm going over to the department, see if I can get a sense of what the committee members are thinking.

EIKO. Look, see, my fingers want to dance — *(She extends them out and wiggles them.)* I need my new piano. Where's my new piano? I want to tickle the ivories! And I can't play on that second-rate one in there.

RAYMOND. I don't know if we can do that right away.

EIKO. We agreed. Raymond? There's a lifestyle I'm introducing you to. A way of life you need to understand and become familiar with if you're going to be a good husband for me.

RAYMOND. Yes, we agreed. Still.

EIKO. What am I? Raymond, what am I? *(Pause.)*

RAYMOND. You're my Japanese American princess. *(Eiko smiles. Raymond exits.)*

EIKO. And all Japanese American princesses must learn to play the piano. Not for fun but for achievement. Not for the love of music but for survival of her species. She's up on a pedestal. La-dee-dah … *(She goes upstage to the* obutsudan, *opens a drawer and takes out a pendant. She opens it and takes out two bright pink pills.)* And the wind cries Mary ... *(Fade to black. A song similar to the Rolling Stones' "Nineteenth Nervous Breakdown" comes up.* We hear the news re: the Vietnam War and student unrest brought up till they are overlapping each other.)*

ACT TWO

*Later that afternoon. Music already playing softly on the
stereo. A song similar to Cream's "White Room."* Eiko brings
in the moving box that she earlier had put away in the back
room. She pauses, goes to the stereo and turns it louder. She likes
it loud. Then goes back to the box and opens it up. Looks at the
contents. Takes out a few albums — Jimi Hendrix, The Beatles,
Blue Cheer, It's A Beautiful Day, Country Joe and The Fish,
Kinks, Them. Picks up a lab beaker.*

*We see a figure peer in from the back window. He watches her
for a beat, then moves away. Eiko hears a noise coming from
the back area and quickly closes the box. She hides next to the
entrance to the living room, waiting for the person to enter.
The song continues to blare over the speakers. As Dr. Nakada
pokes his head out, Eiko grabs him with a trained choke hold.
They shout to be heard over the music.*

DR. NAKADA. Hey, hey, what are you doing?
EIKO. *(Not letting go.)* You shouldn't sneak into my house like
that!
DR. NAKADA. Are you going to release me, Emma Peel? *(Eiko
starts to squeeze tighter.)* I came by to get Raymond for the — This
is not funny, I can't breathe, Eiko! ... *(Eiko lets go. Nakada gasps for
breath.)*
EIKO. If you're going to sneak in the back way, you need to ask
permission.
DR. NAKADA. I had no idea you were so strong.
EIKO. It's technique, purely technique.
DR. NAKADA. Could have fooled me.
EIKO. And this music ... *(Eiko goes to stereo, turns up the volume
even higher. Leans into it with her back to Nakada. The music is rau-
cous. She listens deeply to it, shaking her head frantically. Then she
abruptly shuts it off. Silence.)* It effects me. *(Breathing heavily, looks*

back at Dr. Nakada.) My father wanted to make sure I could defend myself. *(Nakada rubs his neck.)* It could've been much, much worse. I was just practicing.

DR. NAKADA. I won't forget this, Miss Hanabi.

EIKO. And I won't forget what you did to my father.

DR. NAKADA. I think we're both well aware he did it to himself. And where were you all during that time? Off gallivanting around in the Santa Cruz mountains doing God knows what ... *(Pause.)*

EIKO. Would you like some water? *(Nakada straightens his clothes.)*

DR. NAKADA. No. But how about something more interesting?

EIKO. There's no alcohol in the house. I think you know that.

DR. NAKADA. I meant something more interesting.

EIKO. What are you implying? *(He casually takes out a thin hand-rolled marijuana cigarette from his pocket and proceeds to light it. Offers it to her.)* No thanks.

DR. NAKADA. *(Taking a puff.)* Too bad. Maybe you really are more the Pat Boone type. I thought maybe I knew things about you ...

EIKO. And if you did?

DR. NAKADA. Nothing. I'm just a person who likes to know things about people.

EIKO. So you can take advantage of them. Like you did my father.

DR. NAKADA. I did not take advantage of him, I merely spoke his name out loud so everyone could hear.

EIKO. Duke Hanabi was a smart businessman, he founded the Nippon Bank of California —

DR. NAKADA. But in a previous life in Chicago they knew him as Sam Fujita, the infamous dealer of expensive Japanese wares who made his money by stealing antiques from —

EIKO. *(Overlapping.)* He was a shrewd and tough negotiator ...

DR. NAKADA. *(Continuing.)* — the poor Japanese who were so desperate to get food and medicines after the war, they'd take pennies for their most treasured family heirlooms —

EIKO. *(Interrupts.)* All right, all right, enough already ... *(Nakada watches her for a moment, she still looks disheveled and wild.)*

DR. NAKADA. You're bored, aren't you? *(Pause.)*

EIKO. Maybe. Maybe not. *(Beat.)*

DR. NAKADA. How was Japan? I understand they have the gall to speak only Japanese there. Personally I found it exceedingly rude of them.

EIKO. So did I.

DR. NAKADA. And how did Raymond like it? I bet he was in Oriental heaven.

EIKO. Oh, he loved it. Mr. Japanophile himself. He's even taken to wearing a kimono around the house. I don't have the heart to tell him those colors are for an old woman. *(They both find quiet humor in this.)*

DR. NAKADA. Raymond's not a challenge. You need a challenge.

EIKO. A challenge means you have the opportunity to participate. And by participating, an opportunity to win.

DR. NAKADA. Or lose.

EIKO. That wouldn't be so bad. At least I'd be in the game.

DR. NAKADA. I like to win.

EIKO. You have that option. Being in the game is part of your entitlement as a man.

DR. NAKADA. Is that what you want, then? To be a man?

EIKO. I wouldn't mind being a man, the things you're free to do. And not to do. I just have no use for the penis.

DR. NAKADA. Hmm, maybe you're not bored, just frustrated. *(Nakada licks his fingers and tamps out the lit end of the marijuana cigarette, puts it back in his coat pocket.)* You know where you learn the most about people?

EIKO. I'm sure you'll tell me.

DR. NAKADA. In bed.

EIKO. Does that line actually work?

DR. NAKADA. It's not a line, it's the truth. That's why it works.

EIKO. And how does Mrs. Nakada feel about all this truth-telling?

DR. NAKADA. Ahh, the missus.

EIKO. Pretty? Contemporary European Literature? Twenty years your junior?

DR. NAKADA. Amazingly still under the same roof. Still in the same bed.

EIKO. At the same time?

DR. NAKADA. At the same time.

EIKO. And with each other?

DR. NAKADA. We're mature adults. This is the '60s. We have an understanding.

EIKO. Ahhh. An *understanding*. Open marriage, the other professors' wives?

DR. NAKADA. It's been mutually pleasurable. I thought maybe we might have an understanding.

EIKO. I just choked you.

DR. NAKADA. It can lead to orgasm.

EIKO. I heard it led to asphyxiation.

DR. NAKADA. May I have permission to come in the back way? *(Eiko watches him for a bit, as if assessing his sexuality.)*

EIKO. It's a good thing you don't really know anything about me. I'd hate to be in your debt.

DR. NAKADA. I do know you. I just don't know *about* you. Not yet.

EIKO. What's that supposed to mean? *(Nakada moves over to the box he had seen her looking into from the window. He takes out an album and looks at it. A hand mirror. Then a beaker, holds it up and examines it.)*

DR. NAKADA. You were a chemistry major, weren't you? Good mixing up batches of brew. Quite promising, I'm told. *(Eiko takes the beaker and puts the box aside.)* "Why Raymond?" I thought to myself. He's so safe. No, he's not even safe. He's mediocre. Like she's not even trying to run away. She's trying to punish herself. *(Nakada picks up the hand mirror and approaches Eiko. During the following the two move about in a kind of cat and mouse dance, Nakada trying to corner and Eiko continually evading. It has the quality of a dangerous game, mutually pleasureable but with cutting intent. They can be physically rough with each other.)*

EIKO. Not only a swinging professor but a psychic, too?

DR. NAKADA. She's been with any and all the suitors — including that handsome, powerful Kennedy-esque boy — and in the end turned them all away. What does she want? What is she looking for?

EIKO. See, that's the thing about a woman having … *many* suitors. Professor Nakada? He's a man about town. Her? She's someone with a *problem.* That he wants to have an *understanding* with.

DR. NAKADA. She throws up a familiar, though in this case, weak women's liberation rebuttal. Yes, there's truth in what she says. But there are also unsaid truths in what she says.

EIKO. Oh, pray do tell what these are.

DR. NAKADA. She is beautiful, brilliant and, of course, knows it. And yet, her burden is that she also knows she doesn't fit in anywhere. What a cruel fate. Why was she given all this, if she can't really be free to enjoy the fruits of her plentiful gifts? Why?

EIKO. Hmm … *(Nakada has maneuvered himself behind her and holds up the mirror so both their reflections are seen in it. She starts to move but he grips her arm.)*

DR. NAKADA. Because she *sees.* She truly sees her predicament. A few of us are given this horrible gift … *(Eiko pushes him away force-*

fully. He renews his attack.) And so. She chooses to live life like a bat, neither beast nor fowl. The sky is too high, though no one would guess she feels that way, after all she appears to glide so smoothly in that world. And below, the earth — it's the womb from whence she sprang. But that's a second-class world, so how can she live there.

EIKO. *(Sneering.)* I see, above the *white* world and below the *yellow* world …

DR. NAKADA. With her secret festering. Loathing everyone and everything. But most of all, loathing herself. For how can you be free if what you want, you won't let yourself have, and what you don't want, you know you truly are.

EIKO. Ahh, so I settle for less than I want and for more of what I don't.

DR. NAKADA. That way, you lose on all fronts equitably. How egalitarian. Here she is — Mrs. Raymond Pemberthy. Not married to an Oriental, but not married to a real Caucasian man either.

EIKO. I guess you've found me out. *(Eiko moves to the stereo to change the record.)*

DR. NAKADA. Perhaps one day it'll be different. A woman such as you will be able to give herself permission to soar in an arc of total and complete participation. But not right now. Not in 1968. Not for you. Welcome to the world of the bat. *(Nakada moves in close.)* See, we have much in common … *(Eiko cranks up the stereo, a song similar to Blue Cheer's "Summertime Blues."* Nakada pulls back realizing he's been rebuffed. Eiko and Nakada stand staring at each other from across the room while the wall of noise blares.)*

EIKO. You didn't have to tell everyone about my father!

DR. NAKADA. Oh, but I did!

EIKO. Once the Japanese-American community found out who he was they pulled all their money out! He was ruined!

DR. NAKADA. He said Japanese-Americans didn't know how to be real Americans. Look what happened — we all got locked up in camps and he's a rich man with his own bank!

EIKO. I know what you're up to arranging this loan behind my back!

DR. NAKADA. I paid the price to be the real American. I got locked up, not your father, not you, me! I paid the price!

EIKO. Maybe you got my father but you'll never get me, never — *(Raymond bursts in and they stop. He goes over and shuts off the stereo, unsure of what's been going on.)* Oh, hello Raymond.

DR. NAKADA. I came by to get you for the rally.

* See Special Note on Songs and Recordings on copyright page.

RAYMOND. I thought someone was having a party, you could hear it down the street. *(Noticing.)* Was someone smoking in here?

EIKO. I think outside, drifted in through the window ...

RAYMOND. Is everything okay?

EIKO. Yes. Everything is fine.

RAYMOND. I just came from my aunties' house and Auntie Vicky is not doing well.

EIKO. She's always not doing well.

RAYMOND. No, this time it's serious.

DR. NAKADA. I'm sorry to hear that Raymond.

RAYMOND. I stopped by Miles' hotel and he hasn't picked up his note at the front desk, so I don't know. I also had a chance to take a look at Miles' book, they had it on file at the sociology office.

EIKO. And?

RAYMOND. I can see why it went through a mainstream press, it's not really an academic book. It's a kind of a rambling journal of his experiences over the last few years — the whole anti-war thing, psychedelics, the music scene, going underground — an insider's look.

EIKO. So it's not any good?

RAYMOND. No, no I didn't say that. It's just ... different. Different and fascinating. Actually, from what I read, it's very good.

DR. NAKADA. Raymond, you should be careful. It means you'll have to lobby the other members of the hiring committee —

RAYMOND. After they read his work, I don't know if I'll have that much to worry about anyway.

EIKO. It's that good?

DR. NAKADA. You have a paper coming out, don't you?

RAYMOND. A sociological study of the late fifties — changing male and female rituals of the white middle class. Competition brings out the best. And the worst.

DR. NAKADA. Ahh, a person who likes to get in there and muck around, not afraid of what they might find out about themselves.

EIKO. You're hardly making it interesting, Raymond.

RAYMOND. Everyone knew Miles was brilliant but no one thought he'd be able to write down what was going on inside his head — it was so chaotic, out of control —

EIKO. You underestimate yourself. You underestimate me. I am your wife and the competition has hardly begun.

RAYMOND. *(Looking at Nakada, remembering.)* Oh, the administration's big counter-rally we're supposed to go to.

DR. NAKADA. The president made it clear he wanted all faculty, and in Raymond's case, would-be faculty, to be there to support him.

RAYMOND. What if Miles comes by?

EIKO. I'll take care of him if he comes by. Rachel's coming by if anything. And you said yourself he hadn't picked up the message yet.

RAYMOND. That's right. Yeah. But …

EIKO. But nothing, we're all in accord, aren't we?

RAYMOND. Do I have to sit on the stage?

EIKO. Agreed, then. You boys should move along now, we don't want you to be late —

DR. NAKADA. *(Interrupting.)* Actually. We're too early to leave just now. Well. Seeing as we're all agreed and we're still early, let's relax. What shall we do to ready ourselves? *(Dr. Nakada is about to take something out of his pocket when Eiko strides by. She goes straight to the TV and flicks it on, then moves away disinterested. Once again it's about the war in Vietnam, growing involvement and death toll, student unrest. However, world events that are also shaping this period should also be included here. Nakada and Raymond each sit down reluctantly, as if this isn't what they want to be doing. They are quickly drawn in and watch as if in a kind of trance. Eiko refuses to look, with her back to the TV. They hold an informal freeze. This should last for a full thirty seconds. Listening to the news about the war and student unrest and world events. It should be sensorially assaulting — they enter into another zone, lighting shift with a rapid montage of images, exaggerated sounds and news that sum up that particular era in a thirty-second blitz. In some way, this break presages Miles' appearance. Knock at the door. Everything returns to normal. Raymond would like an excuse to get away from the dismal news.)*

RAYMOND. I'll get it! *(Raymond scoots out to the front door. Eiko turns around, watches TV for a beat, then goes to shut it off. Raymond walks in with Miles Katayama. Miles has long wild hair and a quality of erratic genius. Dark sunglasses.)* Look who's here — and no moustache, too! *(Miles stops and looks at Eiko for a long beat.)*

MILES. Hello Eiko.

EIKO. Hello Mr. Katayama.

RAYMOND. This is quite a surprise. We weren't sure whether you got our message or not.

MILES. I phoned in and got them. I've been in meetings all day.

RAYMOND. This is Dr. Nakada, from the business school. *(Shake hands.)*

DR. NAKADA. You do look familiar, have we met?

MILES. Probably seen each other around campus.

DR. NAKADA. What kinds of meetings? *(Beat.)*

MILES. Just meetings.

RAYMOND. Well, I understand you've come back with a bang. I mean, everyone's talking about your book.

MILES. It's not even out yet. And it's not all that interesting.

DR. NAKADA. Why all the false modesty? I hear you sent advance copies to all the major schools. *(Miles takes off his dark glasses. He appears not to know this but feels it's not important enough to address.)*

MILES. Hmm.

RAYMOND. You must be quite proud. I must tell you Miles, I didn't know if you'd ever write again. The circumstances, well, under which you left ...

EIKO. What have you been doing these last few years?

MILES. Thinking. Going places. Visiting unknown countries.

DR. NAKADA. Such as?

MILES. Unfortunately, mostly just in my head, so they'd be of little interest to you. But that's all changed now. I've come back.

DR. NAKADA. Aren't you the least interested in all the happenings on campus? Students protests, anti-war demonstrations, all the Oriental students stirred up. I mean, it was your early activity that helped spawn it.

MILES. You give me too much credit. Besides, my interests are evolving. "Revolution comes from the barrel of a gun"?

DR. NAKADA. Chairman Mao ...

MILES. More like the end of a man's dick.

RAYMOND. Hugh Hefner. *(Silence.)* Joking, joking. *(Beat.)* Oh. Well. Congratulations on your book whenever it comes out. It's a great accomplishment for you.

MILES. The one I'm working on now is the important one. The first book, the one that's coming out, is a rehashing of things I've thought about for a while, I needed to lay the foundation for the new paper. *(To Raymond.)* It's some of the stuff we talked about when we were teaching together — Fanon, colonialism, his theories on race —

RAYMOND. *(Remembering.)* Ah-ah — I still feel racial issues are merely one small component of who and what we are and are being vastly overemphasized in present-day politics —

MILES. Race, the great boogie man of the twentieth century.

EIKO. Do you really believe that, Mr. Katayama?

MILES. The only illusion besides God that makes us kill with conviction and clear conscience.

RAYMOND. Then you agree now — this obsession with what is really only a social construct can only drive us further apart as a society ...

EIKO. What about Fanon's theories on colonized women and their choice of mates?

MILES. I've had discourse in these matters ...

EIKO. How it can lead to complicitous sexualization of the colonizer and desexualization of their own men?

MILES. I have put into action what I believe and opened a few eyes. *(Beat. To Eiko:)* "In all writing I love only what is written in blood ... "

EIKO. Nietzsche.

MILES. *(Answering Raymond.)* If illusion can kill, then race is real enough and must be investigated.

DR. NAKADA. So tell us more about this new paper of yours.

MILES. The one I'm writing now — it's where I begin to decipher the codes — you have to see through the ventriloquism of history, find the linkages. I'm creating a kind of emergency kit for today's living. It isn't meant as a scholarly endeavor but a call to commitment, not an act of writing but writing as an act. There is so little time, so little of us left. I'm trying to grab hold of it, this tiny bit of hope. That we might all get to live a life of uncompromising simple and large truths — a Miles Davis horn riff; a steamy, rich cup of Jamaican Blue Mountain — harvested without tyranny or exploitation; the silky, rhapsodic dimensions of another body that fit so perfectly with yours you no longer know the boundaries of your own flesh ...

EIKO. A kind of *uber*-recipe for liberated everyday living? A space of true spiritual, gender and racial democracy?

MILES. Yes ... For one to eat, another need not go hungry. For one to reap, another need not be forced to bow to the other's will. Why can't we all eat! Why can't we all sleep under a roof and dream the dreams of a mind free!

EIKO. "You have made your way from worm to man."

MILES. Nietzsche.

EIKO. I hope to get a chance to read your new paper some day.

MILES. I've begun to incorporate pre-literate, non-rational arguments, stuff I learned at the the commune I've been living on — intuitive revolution, Zen-Zapata, shoot to vanish stuff — *(Imitating a gunslinger.)* Pow-pow-pow!

EIKO. You're referencing the movie *El Topo*, I take it?

MILES. Jodorowsky, the madman — guns and mysticism, his discussions of the entomological metamorphoses —

EIKO. I do find much of it decadent, slightly misogynist, and at times, quite frankly, obscene — dwarves with no legs ... Mr. Katayama, perhaps "much of you is still the worm."

MILES. I am not the worm. *(Beat.)* It's as if I'm watching an organism grow. Before my eyes. Inside me. At times, my brain feels as if it has a fever ... *(Doorbell rings.)*

EIKO. Raymond, get that. *(Raymond is hesitant but exits. Leaves Miles and Eiko looking at each other. Dr. Nakada stands off to the side observing them.)*

MILES. *(Leans in and whispers.)* Hello Mary.

EIKO. You musn't call me that. It's Eiko Pemberthy now.

MILES. Mary, Mary, quite contrary.

EIKO. *(Out loud for show, moving away from Nakada.)* So Mr. Katayama, I see your work is influenced by the French Caribbean, Frantz Fanon. (Whispering.) Rachel said you were looking for some woman.

MILES. *(Following.)* Rachel? Rachel Cohen? She's here?

EIKO. *(Out loud.)* But do his ideas have relevance to Anglo America? *(Whispering.)* Yes, she's here — she said this woman almost killed you. Is it true?

MILES. *(Out loud.)* Mental illness as a pathology of liberty. *(Whispering.)* I heard it almost killed the woman.

EIKO. *(Whispering.)* Oh really? *(Out loud.)* So you must also examine the cultural and political context of the patient as well. *(Whispering.)* And what else did you hear?

MILES. *(Out loud.)* Yes, sometimes it's the prevailing institutions themselves that must be treated. (Whispering.) I heard they had decided to find out just how deep they could get into each other's heads. They took large doses of this special LSD that they manufactured themselves — and when they got tired, they'd drop some bennies and start all over again. It must've lasted days, maybe weeks —

EIKO. Weeks? I think that's a bit of an exaggeration —

MILES. By the end they'd gone so deep into each other they had lost their individual identities, their separate selves —

EIKO. *(Overlapping.)* This sounds silly —

MILES. — The yin-yang had collapsed, no duality, there was only union.

EIKO. Union?

MILES. Yes, though for some reason she resisted.

EIKO. Maybe it wasn't union for her. Not in the way he thought it was.

MILES. If two people love each other —

EIKO. It was but it wasn't —

MILES. It terrified her, she couldn't handle it, losing herself in another. She started provoking him, hurling despicable, vile insults at him —

EIKO. *(Overlapping.)* This is fucking ridiculous.

MILES. — Which in turn made him do the same to her, making each of them hate each other with equal contempt —

EIKO. Maybe it was the only thing she could do to save herself, to differentiate their identities —

MILES. It set each other off against the other.

EIKO. The psychic divisiveness created psychological division again. She saved their lives.

MILES. She saved herself … *(Silence. Eiko notices Nakada watching.)*

EIKO. *(Out loud.) And how do you like working with Professor Cohen, Mr. Katayama?*

MILES. *(Out loud.) An intellectual pickpocket. (Whispering.)* And I can't believe you're with Raymond. It boggles the mind. I'm amazed there's anything left of him. You should've eaten him alive by now.

EIKO. *(Whispering.)* That's enough. He's a nice fellow.

MILES. *(Out loud.) Where do you think he got his new ideas? (Whispering.)* He's a toad.

EIKO. *(Whispering.)* That's enough, I said.

MILES. *(Moving close to her.)* He's a toad. *(Miles slips his hand beneath her dress.)*

EIKO. *(Weakly resisting, whiles he moves it slowly upwards.)* I like toads. *(Watching each other closely.)*

MILES. There's a small South American frog. Bright yellow. It lives in the humid, tropical rain forest. The poison it excretes — *(Continue.)*

EIKO. *(Overlapping.)* Most amphibian skin toxins are complex nitrogenous compounds. There are much more dangerous poisons called neurotoxins which effect the nervous system — *(Continue.)*

MILES. *(Continuing.)* — from its skin glands against predators and has a bitter, peppery taste that induces vomiting …

EIKO. *(Continuing.)* — some of which can be introduced by the male during sexual activity —*Batrachotoxin*, from the Greek word *batrachos* — frogs, and *toxin* — poison, is one such nerve toxin — in extreme cases known to … *stop the female's heart beating. (Eiko, breathing heavily, pushes his hand away. She sees Nakada watching them and moves away. Raymond enters with Rachel who immediately rushes up to Miles.)*

RACHEL. Oh, Miles, I was so worried about you.

MILES. What are you doing here? Why aren't you up north?

RACHEL. Oh Miles, Miles, you left so suddenly, you didn't even say goodbye to the kids, they were so disappointed.

MILES. I was going to come back and visit as soon as I finished my business here.

RACHEL. Were you really?

MILES. How come you're here? Does Larry have some business down here?

RACHEL. I came down to take care of some business of my own.

MILES. Are the kids with you?

RACHEL. No.

EIKO. I think she was concerned about you. *(Rachel is silent.)*

MILES. I'm fine, I feel better than I have in a long time. *(To Raymond.)* I'm not going after the teaching position. What with the new book I'm working on now, I don't think I'll have a problem getting a position with a prestigious university.

EIKO. Cocky, isn't he?

MILES. *(Glances at Eiko.)* It's the least I could do for you, Mrs. Pemberthy.

RAYMOND. Really? Miles, are you sure?

RACHEL. That gives us more time to work through the ideas we've been struggling with. Make sure they're exactly what you want to say. It'll be so exciting. We're creating something special.

EIKO. How big of you, Mr. Katayama. Isn't it Raymond?

RAYMOND. Well, yes, I'm still a bit stunned. Relieved, I can tell you.

EIKO. Rachel was worried sick about you, that's why she came down, isn't it?

MILES. Is it?

RACHEL. Well …

EIKO. She didn't think you had the strength yet to avoid the temptations that awaited you here.

RACHEL. Eiko, that's not really what I was saying …

EIKO. Your tendency to be rather vulnerable to certain impulses given your fragile nature. After your adventures with Mr. Cohen's "blow-out" therapy? You have a propensity to be — how did you put it? Oh, hell, why not just say it — paranoid?

RACHEL. Eiko …

MILES. Rachel?

EIKO. Certainly given the nature of your close working relationship, these are things you've openly discussed? Or at least, should have? *(To Miles.)* You're upset? Why, considering how much she seems to be sacrificing for you — *(Continuing.)*

RACHEL. *(Overlapping.)* It's not really a sacrifice, I want to do this, it's what I feel I should be doing.

EIKO. — the least you can do is listen to what she has to say. After all, it's for your own good, isn't it?

MILES. What, are you and Larry checking up on me now? How many times have I told you, I'm not going to fall back into my old ways, not this time.

DR. NAKADA. All this truth-telling is making me long for some good ole civilized subterfuge.

EIKO. Lies?

DR. NAKADA. The revelation of truth can be a double-edged sword.

EIKO. Speaking of which … *(Eiko starts to exit.)*

RAYMOND. Honestly Eiko, you're not going to drag *that* out now, are you?

EIKO. *(Calling as she exits.)* When I get paranoid, my weapon of choice.

RAYMOND. *(Calling.)* Eiko, no … *(She ignores him, disappearing into the back room.)* She gets something into her head … *(Awkward silence.)* Well, Dr. Nakada, considering what Miles has told us this evening — *(To Miles.)* and I am certainly in your debt now — maybe I should sit on the stage with the rest of you faculty folks after all. That is, if you are sitting on the stage with President Sommers?

DR. NAKADA. We still have time, this calls for a celebration, given Raymond's newfound respect and station. How about we loosen up a bit before we go over to the admin's rally. Only lies please, only lies …

RAYMOND. I'm sorry, we don't have any alcohol here, Eiko doesn't like to have any around.

DR. NAKADA. I know, I know, Eiko made me aware of this earlier. Might I suggest something less debilitating. *(Pulls out a marijuana cigarette and lights it.)*

RAYMOND. Oh my, oh my … *(Nakada puffs, then holds it out to Miles. Raymond goes over and discreetly closes the window, curtains.)*

RACHEL. I don't think Miles should.

MILES. No thanks. *(He offers it to Rachel who shakes her head. Eiko enters holding a small sword-knife.)*

EIKO. Some prefer pistols. Me? The *aikuchi!* My mother's mother's mother's ...

RAYMOND. Oh, I thought it was on your father's side.

EIKO. *(Does a move.)* Not this. This is from the female side. *(Eiko reaches over, takes the joint and inhales deeply. As if she's been doing it all her life.)*

RAYMOND. Oh my, oh my ...

EIKO. *(Offers it to Raymond.)* Would you care to try some, dear?

RAYMOND. You never cease to ... surprise me.

EIKO. Isn't that why you married me? *(Raymond hesitates.)*

RAYMOND. I thought you didn't drink?

EIKO. I don't.

RAYMOND. I know, I know but it's sort of the same thing, isn't it?

DR. NAKADA and EIKO. No.

EIKO. Besides my not drinking has nothing to do with me.

RAYMOND. *(Taking it.)* I've never done this before.

DR. NAKADA. I think it's pretty evident.

RAYMOND. Like this? *(Inhales like a doofus.)*

DR. NAKADA. Ahh, a natural ... *(Eiko takes it from Raymond and offers it to Miles again. Rachel pulls him away.)*

RACHEL. No, he doesn't want any.

DR. NAKADA. Let's play some billiards. *(To Raymond.)* You any good?

RAYMOND. No.

DR. NAKADA. Perfect, neither am I. How about we wager a little something to make it interesting, say fifty cents a ball ...

EIKO. Lies abound ...

DR. NAKADA. They're more accommodating, aren't they?

RAYMOND. I think I feel something.

EIKO. It's your heart beginning to beat.

DR. NAKADA. Only lies, remember?

RAYMOND. *(Getting an idea, suddenly very excited.)* Hey, hey, hey — the We Five! Let's rock 'n roll!

EIKO. *(Under her breath.)* Oh, my God ... *(Raymond runs over to the stereo and sees Eiko's box. Looks inside and pulls out several albums.)*

RAYMOND. ... The Kinks, Cream, Them, Country Joe, ah-hah — Jimi Hendrix ... *(Calling back.)* Eiko, you never cease to amaze me!

EIKO. That's why you love me, isn't it?

RAYMOND. *(Back to the albums.)* ... Who's Blue Cheer? ... The Beatles! *(Takes the record out.) Magical Mystery Tour*, I loved that movie — Sam Houston Coliseum, 1967. *(Raymond puts on a song similar to The Beatles' "I am the Walrus." Note: at the end of the actual song, it sounds as if there is a phrase being chanted over and over. Music starts, proclaims:)* I am the walrus! *(Raymond joins Nakada in the back room to play billiards. Eiko approaches Rachel and Miles. Miles is irritated with Rachel.)*

EIKO. Belonged to my great-grandmother. A woman can be Samurai, too. They weren't allowed to use the bigger blade, though. Always the short end. Ain't it a bitch being a girl ... *(Starts to demonstrate her skill with the blade.)* "You're such a nice *otonashi* Daddy's girl" — quiet, well-behaved, subservient. "But here in America, remember, you must speak up or you're ignored." But when I open my mouth and say what I think — "Oh no, I'm a castrating American bitch." The worst of the East mixed with the worst of the West ... *(She slashes.)* Better to nod and smile. I haven't the faintest idea what he's saying — nod and smile, nod and smile ... You want to marry me? Nod and smile ... Buy me a house? Nod and smile ... Give you babies? *(Slashes violently.)* It was also used to commit *ojigi*, if you were captured by the enemy. Rather than let yourself be *defiled* by your *husband's rival*, you would kill yourself by doing thus ... *(Demonstrates.)* ... slashing your carotid artery and bleeding to death. But before you did that — this is interesting — you'd tie your legs together, because, God forbid, when you're thrashing around on the ground with blood pouring out of your neck, you should happen to *open your legs*. How indelicate.

MILES. Would you ever consider killing yourself?

EIKO. I've considered killing someone else.

RACHEL. I'm surprised you smoke. I didn't know you did things like that.

EIKO. I did it once a long time ago.

MILES. Why did you stop?

EIKO. Well. Once upon a time, I met someone. And upon meeting him I felt I had met myself for the first time. He could see me, and by seeing me I was cast in the bright light of day. I did not have to be unseen. I heard myself thinking my own thoughts, I spoke my own words, I fought for my territory, I argued my truths. I had never felt that way before. With any man. Especially an Oriental — I mean, Asian man. I was born. But in the end, maybe I was just

* See Special Note on Songs and Recordings on copyright page.

nodding and smiling.

MILES. Is that what you think? *(Raymond runs in with the joint.)*

RAYMOND. *(Holding the joint out to Miles and Rachel.)* Dr. Nakada says we have to share.

EIKO. And wasting my time.

RAYMOND. Miles?

RACHEL. Oh no, Raymond, I don't think it's a good idea.

MILES. Rachel, I can speak for myself. No, not right now. *(Eiko reaches for it and inhales deeply.)*

EIKO. If not now, when?

RAYMOND. *Carpe diem! (Raymond takes a hit and holds it out to Rachel.)*

RACHEL. No, thanks, I'd better not.

MILES. Go on, Rachel. Go on, I can take care of myself.

EIKO. Go on Rachel.

RAYMOND. Yes, Rachel, go on. *(Rachel reluctantly takes a hit.)*

MILES. Is that what things have come to for you? Nodding and smiling and wasting your time?

RAYMOND. You could go to work.

EIKO. *(Affectionately.)* You could go to hell. But that's where you found me, so what's the fun in that, huh?

RAYMOND. You little devil, you ...

EIKO. *(Taking the joint from Rachel.)* I want another hit ... *(Eiko takes a puff and looks at Miles and Rachel. She begins to circle, inspecting them while blowing smoke at Miles.)* Not like you, two, though. Wasting time? No, more like *doing* time. From what Rachel has been saying — locked in your commune hive, busy as worker bees, Rachel buzzing around Miles, taking care of him, bzzz-bzzz, collecting the honey, bzzz-bzzz, storing it in a safe place, bzzz-bzzz —

DR. NAKADA. *(Poking his head out.)* Hey, where is everybody! *(Miles has had enough of Eiko's taunts and snatches the marijuana cigarette from her.)*

RACHEL. Miles, what are you doing?

MILES. *(Pulling Raymond.)* Come on Raymond, let's show them how to really party ... *(Miles takes a hit as he begins to exit with Raymond.)*

RAYMOND. Right on!

RACHEL. *(Starting to follow.)* Miles ...

MILES. *(To Rachel.)* Stay out here. *(Miles and Raymond exit to the back billiards room.)*

DR. NAKADA. *(Offstage.)* All right, another victim!

MILES. *(Offstage.)* Let's do a supercharge!

DR. NAKADA. *(Offstage.)* Oh, my, my, he *has* decided to join the party.

RAYMOND. *(Offstage.)* Hey, Miles is smoking!

RACHEL. Why did you do that? You know it's not good for him.

EIKO. I did it for you.

RACHEL. I'm beginning to think you do everything for yourself.

EIKO. Oh, trust me, I've no interest in Miles. Besides, get too near him and I trust Rachel will sting me dead.

RACHEL. I don't understand you. First I think you want to help us, then it's quite obvious your intentions are anything but.

EIKO. And?

RACHEL. I don't think you even know what you want.

EIKO. Maybe the point is, I want nothing.

RACHEL. Nobody wants nothing.

EIKO. Dead people do.

RACHEL. You're not dead. You want people to think you are. *(The Beatles' song has gotten to the ending where in the background we hear the circular chant "Everybody smokes pot." Dr. Nakada and Raymond come out chanting along excitedly.)*

RAYMOND and DR. NAKADA. *(Chanting.)* ... everybody smokes pot, everybody smokes pot —

DR. NAKADA. It's amazing, Raymond deciphered this — "everybody smokes pot, everybody smokes pot" ...

RAYMOND. *(Demonstrating, chanting enthusiastically.)* "Everybody smokes pot, everybody smokes pot" ...

DR. NAKADA. The Beatles have left a secret message and Raymond's discovered it!

RAYMOND. I'm brilliant! Finally, I'm brilliant!

DR. NAKADA. *(To Raymond.)* You're going a long way in the academic world, buster! *(Miles strides out behind them, pontificating. Raymond continues to excitedly chant along with the record.)*

MILES. *(Over the music.)* — Malcolm X? They killed him. Martin Luther King? They killed him. Bobby Kennedy? They killed him. Bobby Hutton? Dead, murdered, all killed. But look at us. *(To Nakada and Eiko.)* You and me. Buddhaheads. We're still standing, we're still here, we're not dead. Why?

DR. NAKADA. Because we never stick our necks out — we're the model minority!

MILES. Because we don't matter enough! We're not important enough! We're not *dangerous* enough to kill! We must be like our

45

black and brown sisters and brothers who despite the cost of their actions, commit to action thus transforming their acts and themselves in the process. We must — *(Continue.)*

EIKO. *(Overlapping, under the fray.)* … Blah, blah, blah, blah, blah …

MILES. — elevate our consciousnesses by whatever means and become dangerous! *(Continuing. Raymond and Dr. Nakada continue enthusiastically chanting along. They've dragged Rachel away from Miles to join them.)* Otherwise it's just theoretical, existing in the imaginary world where no one grows old and no one dies —

RAYMOND. *(Calling, excitedly.)* The suburbs!

MILES. — *(To Eiko.)* You merely play at life. Not — *(Continue.)*

EIKO. *(Overlapping.)* Blah, blah, blah, blah, blah …

MILES. — participating. Nothing you do is of consequence. You're not dangerous. No love, no revolution. The Brady Bunch. White Face. You. *(Dr. Nakada turns off the stereo.)*

DR. NAKADA. Are we ready?

RAYMOND. We're ready! Fuckin' A we're ready! Bring on the student anti-war demonstrators! All power to the administration! Fuck the students! Fuck Jane Fonda! Fuck Ho Chi Min! Fuck Dr. Spock! Fuck Donna Reed! All power to the faculty! Fuck the students! Fuck me! Yes, fuck us!

MILES. I'm coming, too.

RACHEL. Oh, Miles, I don't think it's a good idea —

RAYMOND and DR. NAKADA. All right!

MILES. I can't miss this, the president speaking to hundreds of pissed-off black, brown and yellow students — And the "Asian-American Students Alliance" might have a surprise in store, too. They've begun to see the connections, the bigger picture — it's not just here, it's about what they're doing to Asians all over the world — Self immolating monks to the *manongs* fighting eviction at the I-Hotel, Hiroshima genocide to the immigrant holding cells at Angel Island. And besides, how could I miss watching Raymond fuck Donna Reed!

RAYMOND. The ground swell of support for — *(Continue.)*

EIKO. *(Overlapping and above the fray.)* Rachel, come over here. Observe, look, look — liberated men off to join the revolution. And what is the position of women in the revolution? To quote Stokely Carmichael, "On their backs!" Yoo-hoo, men, would you like us to serve coffee now? Or how about some cookies and milk for the little warriors before they go off to battle! Would you like some free love now? We're ready to take up our positions for the revolution!

RAYMOND. — the faculty will be enormous. You'll see, you, you Commie-hippie, rebel-rouser — where's your goddamn Fu Manchu moustache! Dr. Lao puts you to shame and he's Tony Randall!

MILES. And you, you old right wing, establishment John Birch buttfucker — we'll see what the students truly think of this outdated, backwards institution of lower learning and what Third World students are capable of when they reclaim their pasts and see the true future!

DR. NAKADA. Lies only lies!

RAYMOND. Fuck Donna Reed!

DR. NAKADA. Me, too! And Jane Fonda, too! *Barbarella* was a great movie! Roger Vadim is God! *(Rachel starts to gather her things.)*

MILES. You stay here.

RACHEL. I want to come.

DR. NAKADA. No girls allowed.

RACHEL. It's *woman*. *(Nakada and Raymond giggle like two school-boys and start to exit.)*

MILES. I'll be back in a few hours. We can drive back up north tonight.

RACHEL. I'm not some little girl. *(Miles starts to exit, Eiko grabs Rachel's arm.)*

EIKO. *(Holding on to her.)* I'll take care of her. You stay here with me.

RAYMOND. *(Calling from off.)* Come on Miles, let's go! *(Miles exits.)*

EIKO. Tell me all the sordid details when you animals get back!

RACHEL. *(Upset.)* Don't you want to go with them? *(Eiko watches her. Then lets her go.)*

EIKO. Okay. I won't stop you. Go.

RACHEL. All right, I will. *(Rachel starts to gather her things again.)*

EIKO. *(Suddenly she speaks forcefully.)* But he doesn't want you to go, Rachel, he doesn't want you to go. *(Beat, conciliatory.)* But go anyway, because that's what *you* want, right? Even if *he* doesn't. After all, it's for his own good. To keep him from fucking up, as it were. *(Now ferocious, closing in on her.)* But isn't he going in the first place because you didn't trust him enough to take care of himself — "He's paranoid, he wants to die," you blathered on — so he got pissed off — and rightly so — and now he's out there and you're in here? So what are you waiting for! Rachel! What are you waiting for? Go! Go! Let's see if you can fuck it up again! *(Rachel breaks down crying. Eiko goes over to the stereo and puts on a song similar to the band Them's "Here Comes the Night."* Then goes and opens the curtains again. Moves back towards Rachel.)* Do you know what a double bind is?

RACHEL. What? *(Eiko ignores her own question.)*

EIKO. You must let him go. Little boys must be allowed to grow up. *(Beat.)* He'll return, you'll see, all grown up in mysterious male ways that you or I will never be allowed to understand. *(Eiko notices something out the window.)* Oh-oh, looks like a tear gas canister. Let the games begin … *(She begins to dance by herself to "Here Comes the Night." She's now holding the small sword. Over the song:)* I'd go. But I don't want to. I want to stay at home *and* want to go. Does that make sense? *(Takes out the sword and whips it around, with skill and precision. It intimidates Rachel. Eiko forces Rachel to dance with her, while still holding the sword. They watch each other closely. Over the music:)* When you can't act but you have to. When you can't scream but you need to. When you can't live but you're simply dying to … *(Points the knife at Rachel's neck.)* Right there. That's where you cut … *(Eiko and Rachel continue to dance. Black out. News comes up overlapping and continues the commentary. Take the act break here. Suggested house music line-up during intermission: Otis Redding, "Dock at the Bay"; Dan Hicks and his Hot Licks, "Canned Music"; Sopwith Camel, "Hello, Hello"; Beau Brummels, "Laugh, Laugh"; James & Bobby Purify, "I'm Your Puppet"; Love, "My Little Red Book"; James Brown, "It's a Man's World."*)*

---

* See Special Note on Songs and Recordings on copyright page.

ACT THREE

As lights fade, a song similar to James Brown's "It's a Man's World" is brought up. * *Dramatic strings begin the song, then into Brown's soulfully ironic chauvinist tribute to women — " ... It's a man's world, but it wouldn't be nothing, without a woman to love a man ... " Then a slow fade as lights come up.*

Just before dawn. Rachel sits up on the couch wrapped in a blanket waiting. Eiko's asleep on the couch snoring lightly. Phone rings in the back room. Eiko gets up and exits to the back to answer it. Eiko reenters moments later.

RACHEL. Was it Miles?

EIKO. No. How did you sleep?

RACHEL. Terrible. I only got a few hours.

EIKO. I slept quite well, thank you. Why don't you go sleep in my bed.

RACHEL. What if he comes?

EIKO. I'll wake you up — go, go. *(Rachel exits into the back room. Eiko is about to put some hot water on when Raymond arrives.)*

RAYMOND. Eiko ...

EIKO. Where are Miles and Dr. Nakada?

RAYMOND. They didn't come by?

EIKO. No.

RAYMOND. I don't know, we got separated. It's been such a strange night Eiko. I'm sorry I stayed out so late but one thing led to another ...

EIKO. What happened?

RAYMOND. Well, the rally was a mess. It never really got started. The Black Student's Union had brought in outside support. A contingent of students — the Asian-American Students Alliance, I think that's what they call themselves — marched right up to the president at the podium with bullhorns, carrying banners — calling for his resignation, saying the university was doing research for a — what'd

---

* See Special Note on Songs and Recordings on copyright page.

they say — a *racist* war, that America was killing Asian people —

EIKO. How did you get separated from Miles and Dr. Nakada?

RAYMOND. Well, when the students started to climb onto the stage, suddenly, out of nowhere, the riot police come storming in — then all hell broke loose. We tried to run away but the police were swinging at everything so Miles just opened the door to this van that was parked there and we all piled in. We surprised a guy and a girl who were in there. We locked the doors, pulled all the shades down and just waited. There was nothing else to do so Miles took his manuscript out from his knapsack and began reading. I'm not sure how long he read, if it was a few minutes or a few hours, they were smoking all this hash, but at one point he stopped, looked up and said it was dedicated to the one great love of his life. And I thought, this could be me talking about you. I mean, if I had written it. We waited till the tear gas cleared up and then we made a run for it. I was the last to leave. That's when we got separated. I looked for them but it was dark and people were still running every which way. I thought maybe they had come back here.

EIKO. I wonder where they went? *(Raymond takes out a manila folder from inside his coat and holds it out.)*

RAYMOND. Look what I found. It's his new paper. Miles'. The one he read to us in the van. He left it behind. Luckily as I was leaving I noticed it. By the time I got outside they were gone.

EIKO. That's it? *(No response.)* Raymond?

RAYMOND. There's something else, too.

EIKO. Yes?

RAYMOND. When Miles was reading it? I felt something quite. Quite, unsettling — ugly, actually. I don't know if I should tell you this. You might think other of me, if I do.

EIKO. *(Getting excited.)* No, no, tell me, tell me Raymond.

RAYMOND. I don't think I want to —

EIKO. *(Almost out of control.)* Tell me! Tell me, Raymond! *(Shocked silence. Raymond is affected by Eiko's excited state.)*

RAYMOND. I felt. I felt all twisted inside because I wished. I wished it was me, not Miles, but me who had written this. I. I found myself envying him with a kind of hateful bitterness — *(Continue.)*

EIKO. Yes, yes …

RAYMOND. — because of what he was capable of doing, this seeming undisciplined, braggard pothead, and maybe I couldn't do it and I wanted to and he didn't deserve to — *(Continue.)*

EIKO. Yes …

RAYMOND. — it should have been me who … *(Silence.)* It's really quite extraordinary. His paper. Wild assertions, at times erratic, and yet …

EIKO. Raymond? Did you really try to find Miles? After you found it?

RAYMOND. What do you mean?

EIKO. It doesn't matter, you're going to get the teaching position, remember?

RAYMOND. Well, yes …

EIKO. Here, give it to me. *(Eiko takes the manuscript and tosses it on the chair.)*

RAYMOND. I have to return it to him, I'm sure he's going crazy if he knows it's gone.

EIKO. Is this the only copy?

RAYMOND. I think so.

EIKO. And no one knows you have it?

RAYMOND. No. *(Beat.)* What a strange night.

EIKO. I have some other news, too. Your Auntie Vicky is very ill.

RAYMOND. When did you hear this?

EIKO. Just before you got here. Your Auntie Gladys called. You should hurry over there.

RAYMOND. She's dying?

EIKO. I believe so.

RAYMOND. Okay, okay, I better go. Did you want to come? It'd mean a lot to Auntie Gladys. And me, too.

EIKO. I really don't think I can handle it, I've been up all night worrying about you and I'm very much out of sorts. I think it's better you go ahead alone. Also, Rachel's sleeping in the back and just in case the rest of them show up …

RAYMOND. Okay, I'll call you later. Where are my things? And, let's see — where's the manuscript?

EIKO. I'll keep it until you get back. Now go, go, you have to hurry … *(Raymond's flustered.)*

RAYMOND. All right …

EIKO. Raymond? I'll take care of everything. *(As Raymond exits, he stops and looks back.)*

RAYMOND. The stakes at which he was writing … Like blood pouring from a wound. I envied him not being white. *(Raymond turns and exits. Eiko goes over and picks up the script.)*

EIKO. We stand so silently. With our breaths held and minds

empty, staring out over the abyss. Waiting. Waiting to be filled with the new knowledge … *(Eiko opens the script and begins to read it. Silence as she becomes absorbed. A knock on the front door, she starts. Eiko hurriedly puts the manuscript in a drawer and goes to see who it might be. She enters with Dr. Nakada who looks quite disheveled.)*

DR. NAKADA. Is Raymond back?

EIKO. Yes — My goodness, Raymond didn't say how bad the strike was. Was anyone hurt?

DR. NAKADA. Oh, this wasn't at the rally. This happened afterwards with Miles. I mean, the rally wasn't a walk in the park. Miles was right, as soon as President Sommers started speaking — well, even before he started speaking — oh, it was a mess. Throwing things at him, at us — your husband talked me into sitting on stage, he's quite persuasive when he's stoned by the way — and you should've seen the students, calling themselves the "Third World" — Negroes, Mexicans, Orientals. I thought they were going to kill us. And I recognized some of them from class — business students! And the Oriental students — I swear they were leading the damn thing — *(Imitating the students.)* "The Vietnamese never called me gook!" What happened to the quiet hardworking model minority? They had approached me a few months ago, wanted to know if I'd be their group's faculty sponsor. I told them maybe they'll change for Negroes but never Orientals. Yellow Power? What the hell is that? More like Yellow Stupid!

EIKO. What about afterwards with Miles?

DR. NAKADA. Oh, yeah, yeah. Anyway, the real trouble started after we got separated from Raymond. Well, actually we ditched him — he's really quite uncool. But Miles — my God, he turns into a raving lunatic, I loved it, I really loved it — he talks me into going over with a couple of the students to the Fillmore, catch the last set of this band he knows. We get over there and he drags me right up to the front of the stage — it's crazier than the riot at the school, only these kids are happy! And the girl, the singer that Miles knows? Beautiful girl, flaming red hair, no bra, see-through blouse — she's singing right to us —

EIKO. *(Impatiently.)* What happened, what happened?

DR. NAKADA. So we get backstage and it's another big party. This time it's nitrous oxide, a huge tank of it, filling up balloons, handing them out —

EIKO. Okay, okay …

DR. NAKADA. Everything's cool. We're all smoking, drinking,

sucking up laughing gas — Miles is chatting with Katey, she's the singer — and, I'm, well, there's this naked girl, just sitting there, in front of me, meditating. But I can tell she's looking at me —

EIKO. Oh, for God's sake Frank, I don't want to hear about your sexual exploits!

DR. NAKADA. Okay, all right, then next thing I know Miles is getting crazy — tearing up the place, he's holding up his knapsack, ranting and raving someone took something out of it. Well, one thing led to another, people start swinging, screaming, the police come — I can hear Miles, "Fuck you pigs! Fuck you pigs!" *(Beat.)* I don't think Miles has to worry about getting a job at State. Ever.

EIKO. Where is he now?

DR. NAKADA. In jail, I imagine. I have to make some phone calls to people, make sure my name is kept out of this. The last thing I need is to have my name attached to Miles and some violent, drug-induced orgy. I'm having nothing to do with that fellow from here on out. You'd better do the same, too, if you want to protect Raymond's teaching position. Have nothing to do with Miles. Especially now. If he comes by, don't talk to him, don't see him, you'll be implicated in this whole sordid mess.

EIKO. Why would I be implicated?

DR. NAKADA. I've been watching you two. There's more here than meets the eye. I can see it. I can smell it.

EIKO. You've a pretty vivid imagination.

DR. NAKADA. I have no imagination, I teach business, remember?

EIKO. Then you're guessing.

DR. NAKADA. *(Grabs her arm forcefully.)* Try me. *(Moves a finger from her neck down to her breast.)* Besides, I have my own personal interests to protect here.

EIKO. You can be quite nasty, can't you.

DR. NAKADA. I told you I wouldn't forget. Your father underestimated me, too.

EIKO. I know how to defend myself, remember? *(During the following speech, Nakada holds Eiko with one hand and moves the other behind her neck.)*

DR. NAKADA. Ahh, that's right, *technique*, the secret language of the privileged, it makes them appear as if their feet don't touch the ground when they walk. I know how to take care of myself, too. I learned at a very special place. Camp Manzanar? For underprivileged Americans? Sent there just as my life and career were about to begin. My style may not be pretty but I know how to get by. Stay low on the radar, don't make waves and you'll be amazed how far they'll let you go. And not go. And I accept that from them — *(During the rest of Nakada's speech, he begins to push Eiko's head down to his groin. She struggles to resist but he is too strong.)* — But it's also allowed me to know and understand people like you, who think they're above all of it. It makes me know that if I'm to get any taste of the real thing, you're the closest I'll ever get to it and if you knew how much I hated being cut off in the middle of my manhood, then you wouldn't be surprised as to how far I'd go to get that taste. *(Nakada releases Eiko's head and she yanks it away.)*

EIKO. You'll always be locked up in Manzanar.

DR. NAKADA. We all have our prisons. Now. I have to go and make sure I've nothing to do with this mess. *(Nakada crosses to leave by the back way. Eiko notices.)* Back door, front door, perhaps soon enough it won't matter. *(He exits. Eiko stands there for a moment. Then remembers Rachel is in the back and goes to check on her. Miles enters through the front door without knocking. He looks haggard, disoriented. Sees Eiko's box and goes over to it. Takes out a chemistry beaker and stares at it. Looks at the records. Pulls an album and puts on a song similar to Jimi Hendrix's "The Wind Cries Mary."* Eiko and Rachel come out. They notice how he looks.)*

RACHEL. Miles? Are you okay?

MILES. No, no I'm not. Hello Eiko. *(He listens to the music.)* It's a nice song, isn't it?

EIKO. I hadn't heard it in a while.

RACHEL. What's wrong Miles?

MILES. Nothing. Everything. We can't see each other anymore. Or rather, I might want to but I don't think you will. Then again, maybe I won't want to see you either. Besides, I've decided to just say, "fuck it." After all, I can't really see anything anymore. *(Points to his eyes and makes them ridiculously big, giggles.)*

RACHEL. What are you talking about?

MILES. My eyes. I haven't mentioned it because it seems too weird but it's as if I went to sleep and woke up with new eyes. I can see patterns and connections and just by closing my eyes I begin to connect the dots, something comes into being. A kind of living picture born of the simple act of *seeing*. Seeing with new eyes.

RACHEL. Yes, yes Miles, that's what we've been doing with your new book, together, and I don't see any reason why we can't continue to do that.

---

* See Special Note on Songs and Recordings on copyright page.

MILES. No, we can't.

RACHEL. Why not?

MILES. Go Rachel, go back to your husband, go back to your children, go back to whatever life it is you had because there is no more you and me, there is no more working together, there is no more new book, I'm not a revolutionary, I'm a fuck-up.

RACHEL. I don't understand.

MILES. *(To Eiko.)* Did you ever want a baby? *(Rachel is confused.)*

EIKO. No.

MILES. *(Back to Rachel.)* I destroyed it.

RACHEL. What?

MILES. The new manuscript. Our work, what we've been doing together. I threw it away, I tore it up — *(Continue.)*

RACHEL. *(Overlapping.)* What are you saying?

MILES. — I burned it, I threw it in the garbage, I flushed it down the toilet, the manuscript, all the ideas, what I was thinking, inside my head, how it all fits together, how it all makes sense —

RACHEL. Why? Why? Why did you do that?

MILES. It's gone, I destroyed it, I killed it, I killed it! *(Rachel stares for a beat, then runs off. Eiko turns off the stereo.)*

EIKO. You talk as if the manuscript was a child.

MILES. These past six months I've been on fire. I write it all down on whatever I can find — napkins, old envelopes, toilet paper — I'm writing, writing … And lo, finally I am change. Now I am revolution. And then I go for a walk down the street and I lose the baby. I'm not change, I'm not revolution. I'm still just a fuck-up! That night? I would've preferred we died then and there. Folded into each other's lives so completely we disappeared. Poof. Perfect.

EIKO. I didn't get scared. I didn't run away. I said those vile despicable things to you because I really meant them. At the point of what you think was complete union, I was fighting with every ounce of my soul to resist. Was I to allow myself to be so overwhelmed by you, absorbed so completely into your identity that I was to be rendered virtually invisible?

MILES. We would disappear together.

EIKO. It's not the same thing for me. What if the worm dies and there is no butterfly yet to emerge? Maybe for the woman it's still unborn, a womb of swirling inchoate ideas and we want it to be there so much we pretend to see what is still not there. Should I still kill the worm? *(Silence. Miles stares at Eiko, then sits down exhausted.)*

MILES. What else can I destroy? What else can I kill? *(Eiko watches Miles.)*

EIKO. Do you mean that? Do you really mean that Miles?

MILES. No book. No Rachel. No Mary. *(Pause.)*

EIKO. There is so little time, there is so little left of us. What do you want? At this moment, what do you really want?

MILES. I want to be gone. Invisible. Perfectly disappeared. I want to be at the place you so hated and reviled. That's where I want to be. *(Eiko watches him for a beat, then takes the pendant out from her blouse. She opens it and takes a pill out.)*

MILES. It's a Mary?

EIKO. The special batch I made. That we took that night. *(He reaches for it but she pulls her hand away, then goes to the windows and slams them open — we hear sirens echoing in the pre-dawn darkness.)* Listen, can't you hear it? *(Sniffing.)* Ahh, the smell of tear gas in the early morning hours! All this chitter-chatter, chitter-chatter, everybody talking, bullshit this, bullshit that — politics, molotovs, SDS, Panthers, priests, *Playboy* bunnies — all transparent, infantalized bullshit. I mean, look where everything you've tried to do has brought you? Self-serving governments still murder cute yellow people, boys still come home in boxes, black people still get lynched, women still bend over for their men and the most potent aphoristic antidote we can come up with is, "Turn on, tune in, drop out"? I mean, in all this muck, what is a truly meaningful action? Huh? What we glimpsed that night. That. Was it merely a spectre of imbibed errant chemicals? A figment of sexual indulgence? Or was it truly a prescient experience?

MILES. Does it matter? You ran away, scared that you'd be swallowed up in my maleness. You were a coward.

EIKO. I ran away because I did not have faith. *(Beat.)* After I left you I wandered with no resistance until the currents of tradition brought me here. The place where no one grows old and no one dies. And then, of my own volition, I stepped up onto the pedestal. Yes, I am a coward. But you don't have to be … "Perfectly disappeared"? You're free to go there. *(Gives him the pill.)* You have a purity, Miles. That's where courage resides. Maybe you just played at life. Maybe you lived a life of no consequence. And maybe you were just a fuck-up. Until now … *(He stares at the pill but doesn't move to take it. Eiko suddenly puts it in her mouth. Then puts her mouth on Miles' mouth in a violent kiss. When she jerks away, it's evident she's passed the pill to Miles. Miles watches Eiko for a moment, then swallows it.) Until now ... (Eiko goes up to the* obutsudan *and retrieves a bundle wrapped up in a white cloth. She brings it back to Miles who opens it up. It's the* aikuchi.) In a time of moral ambiguity, the freedom fighter addresses himself and no one else. A pure act — absolute, unequivocal, final — is the gesture of the hero. *(Miles does not respond.)* A pure act.

MILES. Eiko?

EIKO. I cannot go with you. But let me be with you. Do you understand? *(No response.)* Do you understand?

MILES. Yes.

EIKO. Do you promise? *(Long pause.)*

MILES. With this act, finally I am action.

EIKO. Yes, yes ...

MILES. Now, I am revolution.

EIKO. Now, we are union. *(Miles wraps up the* aikuchi.*)* I won't go looking for you.

MILES. I won't tell you where I go. Goodbye Mary.

EIKO. Do it ... beautifully. *(He leaves. Eiko shuts the door and stands there in silence for a moment. Then goes to the stereo and puts on a record. A song similar to "White Bird" by the band It's A Beautiful Day.* Goes to the drawer and takes out the manuscript. She sits by the fire and holds it.)* We stand so silently. With our breaths held and minds empty, staring out over the abyss. Who will give us wings ... *(Miles lit with the* aikuchi.*)*

MILES. *(Musing, he's high on the hallucinogen.)* Revolution. Revolution. Revolution ... *(Thinking.)* Evolution. Evolution. Evol ... E-V-O-L. L-O-V-E ...

EIKO. Love ...

MILES. I am dangerous, I am dangerous, I am dangerous ... *(Miles blacks out. Eiko tears off the page and throws it into the fire.)*

EIKO. *(Begins reciting.)* D-lysergic acid diethylamide — carbon 20, hydrogen 25, nitrogen 3, oxygen. Molecular weight 323.43. Administered, oral. Threshold dose — 10-50 micrograms. But the average "hit" sold on the street is typically around 250 micrograms ... *(Eiko tears off another, then more, gathering momentum and fury as she continues to recite the chemical properties of LSD. More news of Vietnam and campus strife. The song swells. Blackout.)*

---

* See Special Note on Songs and Recordings on copyright page.

ACT FOUR

The room is in shadows. Auntie Gladys and Eiko sit across from each other. Both dressed in black. Awkward silence. Eiko fidgets. Auntie Gladys is composed.

EIKO. He said he was coming right here?
AUNTIE GLADYS. We took two cars so he didn't have to drive me back. He was following me. *(Noticing Eiko.)* It's amazing.
EIKO. What?
AUNTIE GLADYS. Even in funeral black you look good.
EIKO. He called from your place and said you were coming so I put this on ...
AUNTIE GLADYS. *(Marveling.)* How do you do it? *(Beat.)*
EIKO. So she died peacefully?
AUNTIE GLADYS. Yes. Quite beautiful actually. That's the way I want to go. Do you have any more of those chocolates I brought over?
EIKO. *(Realizing she hasn't offered anything.)* Oh, I'm sorry, would you like some tea or coffee or something? *(Eiko puts a pot of water on the stove.)*
AUNTIE GLADYS. I asked for chocolates. Remember the cheap ones I brought over?
EIKO. Oh. *(She looks in a drawer and returns with a box of chocolates.)*
AUNTIE GLADYS. What are these?
EIKO. Conrad Schmitz. Truffles.
AUNTIE GLADYS. What happened to the nougats I brought?
EIKO. Try one.
AUNTIE GLADYS. You threw them out didn't you?
EIKO. Try one. *(Eiko holds them out. Beat. Auntie Gladys cautiously takes a truffle. Stares at it skeptically.)* Come on, come on. *(She takes a nibble.)* Over the mouth and through the gums —
AUNTIE GLADYS. Oh, shut up. *(Eiko smirks. Auntie Gladys chews.)*
EIKO. You like?
AUNTIE GLADYS. They're all right.

58

EIKO. You like?

AUNTIE GLADYS. Not bad.

EIKO. Well, then … *(She starts to take the box away when Auntie Gladys stops her.)*

AUNTIE GLADYS. Why don't you just leave them for now.

EIKO. But I thought you didn't —

AUNTIE GLADYS. Leave them.

EIKO. But you said —

AUNTIE GLADYS. Please, leave them.

EIKO. *(Watches her for a beat.)* Okay … *(Eiko sets them down and sits back down opposite her. Auntie Gladys takes a truffle and pops it whole into her mouth. She slowly chews it savoring its flavor.)*

AUNTIE GLADYS. Ahhh … *(Auntie Gladys seems revived now.)* I had to come over here. Funny, huh? Auntie Vicky's just passed away and I say to Raymond, "Quick, we must go over and tell Eiko." He says why not just phone her and I say, "No, no, we got to go over there, to the house, I need to tell her in person." So here I am and I'm not sure why I'm here … *(Raymond has just entered and heard the last part.)*

RAYMOND. Sorry, I'm late getting here. I had an errand to run before I came home. *(Kisses Auntie Gladys.)* I'm sure Eiko appreciates your thoughtfulness.

EIKO. Yes, I do appreciate you coming over and telling me in person.

AUNTIE GLADYS. It's so odd how things happen. One life leaves just as another arrives. Maybe that's why I'm here. To let you know in person that the one who's going to die, has. So the one who's supposed to arrive, can.

RAYMOND. Auntie?

AUNTIE GLADYS. What am I going to do now? What am I going to do? Maybe Auntie Vicky was the lucky one. She gets to leave first. Not be left alone. I've been taking care of her for the last twenty years, I don't know what else to do. Who am I going to care for?

EIKO. She liked the truffles.

RAYMOND. Oh. Would you like us to order you some?

AUNTIE GLADYS. They're very expensive, aren't they?

RAYMOND. It's okay, Auntie. After all, you're all I have left.

AUNTIE GLADYS. And you two are all I have left. Maybe there's something I can help you with. You're going to be needing an extra hand and that's right up my alley.

EIKO. They're from Chicago. The truffles. A small boutique shop.

We have them sent over from there.

RAYMOND. Why don't you stay here for a while, you don't have to go right back. The doctor's over there and he said it would take a while for the ambulance to arrive. Seeing as it really isn't an emergency ...

AUNTIE GLADYS. Auntie Vicky was really worried about Hop Sing. She was. Wrote a letter to the TV station and everything. Now that Eiko was with you, Auntie Vicky felt it her duty to understand her people better. That's why we had to watch *Bonanza*. Where did Hop Sing sleep? In the kitchen? They never say. In the bunkhouse with the other cow pokes? Vicky didn't think they'd want him in there with them. "Poor Hop Sing," she'd say. *(Beat.)* It's so odd, like she was just sleeping, you know. Like she was going to wake up any moment, just like always. But when I walked over and touched her ... *(Auntie Gladys acts it out, her hand extending. She holds it for a beat as both Eiko and Raymond watch her. Then she pulls it back and becomes herself again.)* When someone close leaves us, it's comforting to know that another will soon arrive.

EIKO. Would you please stop talking so cryptically, it's making me sick.

RAYMOND. Eiko, please. *(Awkward pause. Eiko goes to the window and looks out.)*

AUNTIE GLADYS. Well, I better be going. I really should be there when they take Vicky away.

RAYMOND. You sure you don't want to stay a bit?

AUNTIE GLADYS. *(Shakes her head.)* They're both gone now — first your father, and now Vicky. *(Beat.)* Why did I have to come here? *(She turns to leave.)*

EIKO. *(Not looking from the window.)* Goodbye Auntie Gladys. *(Auntie Gladys stops and turns around to look at Eiko. Raymond, too, is surprised by Eiko calling her by "Auntie." Eiko turns to look at them both.)*

AUNTIE GLADYS. I wondered why ... *(Auntie Gladys walks over to Eiko, stopping in front of her. She looks at Eiko for a moment, then slowly reaches out and touches her naked arm, and holds it there as if feeling something. Then she withdraws it, turns and leaves. She's her old self again. She grabs the box of truffles as she exits. Calling loudly as she exits:)* You two have things to talk about. And Raymond? Maybe Eiko has something to tell you. *(Stops at the door.)* I said to Auntie Vicky, "Who cares?" He has a good thing and he knows it. This was the goddamn Ponderoza for criminy sakes! *(Raymond sees*

Auntie Gladys out. Eiko is feeling her arm where she was touched. Raymond returns.)

RAYMOND. That was nice of you to call her Auntie Gladys. I'm still really worried, though.

EIKO. She'll be fine. She's as strong as a horse.

RAYMOND. No, I mean, about Miles.

EIKO. Do you have any news?

RAYMOND. I stopped over his place on the way here, I wanted to tell him we had the manuscript.

EIKO. Did you see him?

RAYMOND. No, he wasn't there, but as I was leaving I ran into Rachel. She said Miles stopped by here last night.

EIKO. Yes, after you left.

RAYMOND. She said Miles told her he'd destroyed the manuscript.

EIKO. Yes.

RAYMOND. My God, he must be truly losing it. So you didn't tell him you had it?

EIKO. In the state he was in? I didn't think it was the prudent thing to do. Did you tell Rachel we had it?

RAYMOND. No. *(Awkward silence. They look at each other.)* I was a bit confused because of what Rachel said Miles told her about the manuscript. I know they were here and I assumed you were present when he said what he said, I didn't understand what was going on. But. Maybe you should have told Miles. You know, when he came over? *(Eiko remains silent.)* Well, I better take it over to him now. In his state he might do anything. Where is it? Eiko?

EIKO. I don't have it.

RAYMOND. You don't have it?

EIKO. No.

RAYMOND. Well, where is it then?

EIKO. I burned it.

RAYMOND. What?

EIKO. I burned the manuscript. Last night.

RAYMOND. Miles' paper? What — you burned it? Why would you burn it?

EIKO. I wish I had a Conrad Schmitz truffle.

RAYMOND. Are you insane? You burned his manuscript? It wasn't yours to do that to. It's Miles'. My God, this could get us in a lot of trouble, Eiko. That was the only copy, you know. That was it. The whole paper, gone, you destroyed a major work. What in the world possessed you to do —

EIKO. I did it for you. *(Pause.)*

RAYMOND. What?

EIKO. For you. That's why I destroyed his manuscript.

RAYMOND. What are you talking about?

EIKO. You said you envied his work. Envied him.

RAYMOND. Yes, but ...

EIKO. This way you don't have to worry about him. His competition. You, my husband, are alone at the top of the heap.

RAYMOND. For me? You did that for me? But what if someone finds out?

EIKO. Who's going to find out? No one knows you found it, right?

RAYMOND. No.

EIKO. I didn't tell anyone. So ... *(Raymond is speechless.)* So you publish your new book. It comes out. It gets the full attention it deserves. Not more, not less, but exactly what it should rightfully get. Let it stand or fall on its own merits. But let's not have these other people's works floating about to detract from its deserved consideration.

RAYMOND. Eiko? You did that for me? But. I don't know what to say.

EIKO. Say, "Thank you!" Thank you my wife for having the balls to do something that will actually help me in my career, my life! But. Do tell me. You weren't thinking just a little along the same lines, I mean, why did you bring the manuscript back home in the first place? And why didn't you tell Rachel what really happened to Miles' manuscript when you just saw her? Huh? *(Raymond is silent.)* But these are things you needn't worry your pretty head about because I've taken care of them for you. For you! For you!!! *(Raymond doesn't know what to say. Eiko goes over to the stereo and puts on a song similar to The Kinks' "You Really Got Me."* Loud. Talking over the music:)* And you know what else I've done for you? Know what else? Check out my profile. Notice anything? You crawl all over me every night, poking me, biting me, sticking me — didn't you feel anything different? My waist getting wider? My ass a bit larger? My nipples a little harder? Doesn't it seem to be all swelling up like a spoiled cabbage?

RAYMOND. You don't mean? You mean, you're pregnant? You are?

EIKO. I'm fat! I'm fat!

RAYMOND. Oh, Eiko, this is wonderful, this is truly a miracle! *(Music blaring.)*

---

* See Special Note on Songs and Recordings on copyright page.

EIKO. It's killing me! It's killing me!

RAYMOND. Having a baby is wonderful, it's not going to kill you! *(A winded Rachel bursts in.)*

RACHEL. I had to come over. *(Raymond turns off the stereo.)*

RAYMOND. Rachel?

RACHEL. I was over at the faculty housing and I overheard someone say Miles was in the hospital. That he had some kind of accident.

RAYMOND. What happened? Is it serious?

RACHEL. I don't know. That's why I came over here to see if you knew anything.

EIKO. No, we've heard nothing.

RACHEL. I have this bad feeling, this very bad feeling. I heard what happened last night at the Fillmore and how he got arrested. He went to see that woman. Have any of you seen him? Did he stop by again?

EIKO. No.

RAYMOND. The last we've heard of him was when he stopped by and talked to both of you. *(Nakada bangs on the back window. And then hurries around and enters from the back. Dressed in a dark suit, carrying his briefcase.)*

DR. NAKADA. Well, everyone's here. Oh, I'm sorry about your aunt, Raymond.

RAYMOND. That's okay, thank you.

RACHEL. Do you know something about Miles?

DR. NAKADA. Oh, so you've heard?

RACHEL. Just that he had an accident and he's in the hospital.

DR. NAKADA. Nothing else?

RAYMOND. No.

DR. NAKADA. He is in the hospital. It's very serious. *(Beat.)* He may not recover.

RACHEL. *(Overwhelmed.)* Oh Miles, I knew it, I knew it … *(Raymond helps her to the couch. Eiko removes the pendant from around her neck and lays it on the* obutsudan. *Nakada notices.)*

EIKO. What kind of accident?

DR. NAKADA. He was stabbed.

RAYMOND. Oh, my God. How did that happen?

DR. NAKADA. He got into a fight it seems.

RACHEL. Oh Miles, I knew he was going to get himself into trouble. I knew it …

DR. NAKADA. *(To Eiko.)* Do you know anything about this?

EIKO. Why would I?

DR. NAKADA. I thought you might.

EIKO. I can't say it's unexpected.

DR. NAKADA. And what do you mean by that?

EIKO. Perhaps he has fooled all of us. Fooled you, Nakada. An *accident?* Perhaps Miles found his manhood and committed a willful, intentioned act. And as such, it was anything but an accident. *(Raymond goes to get Rachel some water.)*

RAYMOND. *(Noticing.)* Your hot water, Eiko. *(Eiko goes over and shuts it off. Nakada has been watching her.)*

RACHEL. Maybe I should go over there.

DR. NAKADA. I don't think it's wise, right now.

RAYMOND. Just rest here for a bit. He's at the hospital, I'm sure they're doing everything they can. We can phone over later and check.

RACHEL. What about his manuscript? Did he really destroy it?

DR. NAKADA. It wasn't found with him, as far as I know. Do you folks know anything about it?

RAYMOND. Why, no.

DR. NAKADA. It's a shame, from what he read to us, it was quite original. *(Raymond looks at Eiko.)*

RACHEL. I can't believe there's nothing of the work we did together. Nothing.

RAYMOND. You said something about having some notes, right?

RACHEL. Yes, in my knapsack.

RAYMOND. Well, let's look at them. It's a long shot but maybe there's a way we can reconstruct some of the more important ideas.

EIKO. Raymond?

RAYMOND. I mean, we were trapped for a whole two and a half hours while he read chapter headings and then did extemporaneous synopses of their contents.

EIKO. You said you didn't remember how long?

RAYMOND. And this one, like his book, it isn't an academic work, footnoted all over the place. It's more a visionary stream of consciousness …

RACHEL. Do you think it's actually possible to recreate the work?

RAYMOND. Of course not in entirety, but maybe we can put together enough to publish some smaller papers on selective topics. Let's see the notes you have … *(Nakada goes to Eiko who stands off to the side.)*

DR. NAKADA. I was fooled, huh?

EIKO. Miles finally found his courage. Tell me how it happened. I want to know every last detail.

DR. NAKADA. You are more dangerous than I thought.

EIKO. A kind of purity to leave on one's own terms, don't you think?

DR. NAKADA. He turned up at another students rally over at Berkeley. They let him speak because of who he was but he was incoherent — babbling on and on about how one day it's going to be hip to be Asian in America — white kids in suburbs eating raw fish, black inner city kids idolizing Japanese ball players. The students laughed him off the stage. Then later he turned up at the house where that band was staying. It's a known drug hangout. Seems he was still looking for whatever he thought they stole from his knapsack. He went straight to the singer's bedroom. This time she was sober and wasn't about to put up with his antics. And given his state of mind. Seems there was a struggle —

EIKO. And she stabbed him?

DR. NAKADA. More or less.

EIKO. What do you mean?

DR. NAKADA. It was in the groin. Or more specifically, she cut off his penis. *(Silence. Eiko is stunned, physically revolted.)* I believe you're right. It couldn't have been an accident. Her aim was far too good. It's like a very bad joke and I didn't want to mention it in front of Rachel. He lost too much blood. He died on the way to the hospital.

EIKO. *(Recovering. To herself.)* A worm is a worm is a worm ... *(Nakada goes to the* obutsudan *and picks up the pendant. He finds a pill inside.)*

RAYMOND. *(Excitedly.)* Hey, I think we'll be able to put together the first chapter!

RACHEL. Yes, I know we can do it! *(Eiko has moved up to the kitchen to make her tea. Nakada joins her with his briefcase.)*

DR. NAKADA. *(Holding out the pill.)* There'll be an autopsy. Test his blood. And if they find any controlled substances, given the nature of his death, I'm sure they'll want to know from whom he got it. These *Marys* as they were fondly called by their *maker*.

EIKO. Really? *(Eiko pushes by him and crosses down to get the tea she'd put away earlier. Dr. Nakada takes something wrapped in a cloth out of his briefcase and follows Eiko downstage. He pulls out the* aikuchi *from the bloodied white cloth and shows it to Eiko.)*

DR. NAKADA. As I mentioned, I have friends down at the department. *(Beat.)* I asked them if given all these circumstances, could criminal charges be brought? They said without question.

We're looking at an indictment, a very public trial and more than likely the humiliation of prison. *(Silence.)*

EIKO. *(Notices the weather outside.)* Such a beautiful day for a funeral. I was a very little girl when my mother died. Everything was white.

DR. NAKADA. It's the color of death in Japan.

EIKO. Only it's not really a color, is it? All I have left of her is that lone knife. *(Eiko reaches for the* aikuchi *and Nakada pulls it away.)* I feel you do know things about me now.

DR. NAKADA. I believe I might.

EIKO. I think I know what you're asking of me, Professor Nakada.

DR. NAKADA. Yes?

EIKO. Yes.

DR. NAKADA. Do we have an understanding?

EIKO. We do.

DR. NAKADA. We're the last of our breed. You and me. Bats. It's a whole new world now. At least for the younger ones. Not us, though. We've made our choices. And we have to live with them. *(Silence. Eiko holds out her hand. Nakada is hesitant.)* The back door, the front door, are always open. We have an understanding?

EIKO. We have an understanding. *(Nakada drops the pill into her hand. Eiko keeps it extended, wanting the* aikuchi *also. Nakada cautiously places the knife-sword into her hand, holding his hand over hers.)*

DR. NAKADA. A gentleman's agreement, then.

EIKO. Yes, a *gentleman's* agreement. *(He releases the sword.)* At last, I'm on equal terms. *(Eiko moves to the shrine and places the* aikuchi *there in a reverent manner.)*

RAYMOND. Eiko, I think we might be able to do this. Well, not reconstruct the whole thing, but Rachel's notes are quite extensive and very detailed.

RACHEL. Oh, no, I wouldn't know what to do with them without Raymond.

RAYMOND. This is a very important work, a major opus and we must do everything we can to salvage it. *(Eiko moving to them. To Rachel:)* What does that line mean, the "thought unknown"?

RACHEL. A vision he had with that woman — we'll have to go back and see if we can cross-reference it, find out its meaning that way …

EIKO. Is there anything I can help you with?

RAYMOND. What? Oh, no, there's nothing you can do. Besides, you must rest, remember? Why don't you go keep Dr. Nakada company. *(They return to their work. Nakada smiles at her.)*

DR. NAKADA. How about some music? Something to soothe the nerves. *(Eiko thinks for a beat, then moves to the stereo. She puts a record on and steps off to the side looking out the downstage window. It's a song similar to Jimi Hendrix's "Purple Haze" — extremely loud.*)*

RAYMOND. What the — Eiko! Eiko! *(Raymond runs over and turns the music off.)*

EIKO. Yes?

RAYMOND. You can't play the music so loud when we're trying to work.

EIKO. Yes, dear.

RAYMOND. You were heating up water weren't you — Make us some tea.

EIKO. How about coffee?

RAYMOND. Tea, Eiko. *(Returning to Rachel.)* Why don't you move in to my Aunt Gladys' place, that way you'll be closer so we can continue the work.

RACHEL. Oh, yes, yes, wonderful — Auntie Gladys won't mind?

RAYMOND. She'd love your company. And the kids, too. *(They resume. Eiko watches them for a beat. She looks around. Then announces:)*

EIKO. Attention. I'm making tea for everyone. *Mugi-cha!*

DR. NAKADA. Wonderful idea. Wonderful idea. I love *mugi-cha.*

RAYMOND. Hey, how ironic, I become the voice for Asian-American students. Fanon would have a field day with this one!

DR. NAKADA. Maybe I'll be their faculty sponsor. *(A song similar to Erik Satie's "Trois Gymnopedie" comes on.* Lighting shift so Eiko is highlighted in a pool of light. Eiko makes the tea. She places the Mary, the LSD pill, in the pot. Swirls it around. Pours out the tea into four cups. Then gets up and serves the tea on a tray.)* I'm feeling at home already.

EIKO. Tea?

DR. NAKADA. *(Takes a cup.)* The first of many, I assume. *(Eiko brings tea over to Raymond and Rachel. They both take the tea without acknowledging her presence. She returns to her original position and sits down in front of her lone remaining tea cup. The following has an intentioned, deliberate quality, bordering on ritual. As she brings the tea cup to her lips we sense she is coming to a decision. She stops, the cup held in mid-air. Then, slowly, she turns the cup over pouring the tea onto the ground. She then places the teacup back on the tray, upside*

---

* See Special Note on Songs and Recordings on copyright page.

down. Music stops. A beat. She gets up and moves with a quiet measured walk up to the shrine. She takes the aikuchi *in both hands and stands there for a moment with her head bowed. Eiko then returns and sits down on the sofa with the knife-sword in her lap. She looks around taking in the scene. Raymond and Rachel, engaged in their work. Then at Dr. Nakada who appears lost in his own thoughts and unaware of Eiko. It could be a day like any other normal day. Eiko looks straight ahead for a moment. Then she takes the* aikuchi *in hand.)*

EIKO. *(Proclaiming.)* My legs are unbound! *(Eiko slashes her throat and immediately places her hand on her neck. With tremendous will she stays erect. Rachel sees her and screams.)*

RAYMOND. My God, what have you done? *(Eiko slowly takes her hand away revealing a bloodied neck. She maintains this pose for a beat, as if defying the moment and proclaiming her victory to the others. She collapses, her legs sprawled open.)*

DR. NAKADA. No, no, no ... *(Slow fade to black. A song similar to "Ferry Cross the Mersey" by Gerry and the Pacemakers is brought up.* Underneath it we hear the news report. Something that completes the arc and posits the irony of the story's narrative, spins it off into the next step. E.g. the Administration capitulates, the progressive President Sommers has quit, the conservative S.I. Hayakawa is now installed. And, that the Ethnic Studies Department has been established with divisions of Black American, Chicano and Asian-American Studies established. The war rages on, the body count rises.)*

End of Play

PROPERTY LIST

We Five album (RAYMOND)
Canister of tea, teapot (RAYMOND)
Serving tray, pot of water (RAYMOND)
Box of chocolates (AUNTIE GLADYS, RAYMOND, EIKO)
Folded note (AUNTIE GLADYS, RAYMOND)
Storage box with albums, lab beaker (EIKO, MILES)
Instant coffee, cup (EIKO)
Knapsack (RACHEL)
Pendant with two pink pills (EIKO, DR. NAKADA)
Marijuana cigarette, lighter (DR. NAKADA, RAYMOND)
Album, hand mirror, beaker (DR. NAKADA)
Small sword-knife (EIKO, DR. NAKADA)
Albums (RAYMOND)
Blanket (RACHEL)
Pot of water (EIKO)
Manila folder of paper (RAYMOND, EIKO)
Box of truffles (EIKO, AUNTIE GLADYS)
Briefcase (DR. NAKADA)
Glass of water (RAYMOND)
Pink pill (DR. NAKADA, EIKO)
Teapot, tray, four cups (EIKO)

SOUND EFFECTS

Songs on stereo
News bites: American troop activity in Vietnam, student unrest
Knock at the door
Piano notes
Doorbell
Phone ring
Sirens

NEW PLAYS

★ **BE AGGRESSIVE by Annie Weisman.** Vista Del Sol is paradise, sandy beaches, avocado-lined streets. But for seventeen-year-old cheerleader Laura, everything changes when her mother is killed in a car crash, and she embarks on a journey to the Spirit Institute of the South where she can learn "cheer" with Bible belt intensity. "…filled with lingual gymnastics…stylized rapid-fire dialogue…" –*Variety*. "…a new, exciting, and unique voice in the American theatre…" –*BackStage West*. [1M, 4W, extras] ISBN: 0-8222-1894-1

★ **FOUR by Christopher Shinn.** Four people struggle desperately to connect in this quiet, sophisticated, moving drama. "…smart, broken-hearted…Mr. Shinn has a precocious and forgiving sense of how power shifts in the game of sexual pursuit…He promises to be a playwright to reckon with…" –*NY Times*. "A voice emerges from an American place. It's got humor, sadness and a fresh and touching rhythm that tell of the loneliness and secrets of life…[a] poetic, haunting play." –*NY Post*. [3M, 1W] ISBN: 0-8222-1850-X

★ **WONDER OF THE WORLD by David Lindsay-Abaire.** A madcap picaresque involving Niagara Falls, a lonely tour-boat captain, a pair of bickering private detectives and a husband's dirty little secret. "Exceedingly whimsical and playfully wicked. Winning and genial. A top-drawer production." –*NY Times*. "Full frontal lunacy is on display. A most assuredly fresh and hilarious tragicomedy of marital discord run amok…absolutely hysterical…" –*Variety*. [3M, 4W (doubling)] ISBN: 0-8222-1863-1

★ **QED by Peter Parnell.** Nobel Prize-winning physicist and all-around genius Richard Feynman holds forth with captivating wit and wisdom in this fascinating biographical play that originally starred Alan Alda. "QED is a seductive mix of science, human affections, moral courage, and comic eccentricity. It reflects on, among other things, death, the absence of God, travel to an unexplored country, the pleasures of drumming, and the need to know and understand." –*NY Magazine*. "Its rhythms correspond to the way that people—even geniuses—approach and avoid highly emotional issues, and it portrays Feynman with affection and awe." –*The New Yorker*. [1M, 1W] ISBN: 0-8222-1924-7

★ **UNWRAP YOUR CANDY by Doug Wright.** Alternately chilling and hilarious, this deliciously macabre collection of four bedtime tales for adults is guaranteed to keep you awake for nights on end. "Engaging and intellectually satisfying…a treat to watch." –*NY Times*. "Fiendishly clever. Mordantly funny and chilling. Doug Wright teases, freezes and zaps us." –*Village Voice*. "Four bite-size plays that bite back." –*Variety*. [flexible casting] ISBN: 0-8222-1871-2

★ **FURTHER THAN THE FURTHEST THING by Zinnie Harris.** On a remote island in the middle of the Atlantic secrets are buried. When the outside world comes calling, the islanders find their world blown apart from the inside as well as beyond. "Harris winningly produces an intimate and poetic, as well as political, family saga." –*Independent (London)*. "Harris' enthralling adventure of a play marks a departure from stale, well-furrowed theatrical terrain." –*Evening Standard (London)*. [3M, 2W] ISBN: 0-8222-1874-7

★ **THE DESIGNATED MOURNER by Wallace Shawn.** The story of three people living in a country where what sort of books people like to read and how they choose to amuse themselves becomes both firmly personal and unexpectedly entangled with questions of survival. "This is a playwright who does not just tell you what it is like to be arrested at night by goons or to fall morally apart and become an aimless yet weirdly contented ghost yourself. He has the originality to make you feel it." –*Times (London)*. "A fascinating play with beautiful passages of writing…" –*Variety*. [2M, 1W] ISBN: 0-8222-1848-8

DRAMATISTS PLAY SERVICE, INC.
440 Park Avenue South, New York, NY 10016 212-683-8960 Fax 212-213-1539
postmaster@dramatists.com www.dramatists.com

NEW PLAYS

★ **MONTHS ON END by Craig Pospisil.** In comic scenes, one for each month of the year, we follow the intertwined worlds of a circle of friends and family whose lives are poised between happiness and heartbreak. "...a triumph...these twelve vignettes all form crucial pieces in the eternal puzzle known as human relationships, an area in which the playwright displays an assured knowledge that spans deep sorrow to unbounded happiness." *–Ann Arbor News.* "...rings with emotional truth, humor...[an] endearing contemplation on love...entertaining and satisfying." *–Oakland Press.* [5M, 5W] ISBN: 0-8222-1892-5

★ **GOOD THING by Jessica Goldberg.** Brings us into the households of John and Nancy Roy, forty-something high-school guidance counselors whose marriage has been increasingly on the rocks and Dean and Mary, recent graduates struggling to make their way in life. "...a blend of gritty social drama, poetic humor and unsubtle existential contemplation..." *–Variety.* [3M, 3W] ISBN: 0-8222-1869-0

★ **THE DEAD EYE BOY by Angus MacLachlan.** Having fallen in love at their Narcotics Anonymous meeting, Billy and Shirley-Diane are striving to overcome the past together. But their relationship is complicated by the presence of Sorin, Shirley-Diane's fourteen-year-old son, a damaged reminder of her dark past. "...a grim, insightful portrait of an unmoored family..." *–NY Times.* "MacLachlan's play isn't for the squeamish, but then, tragic stories delivered at such an unrelenting fever pitch rarely are." *–Variety.* [1M, 1W, 1 boy] ISBN: 0-8222-1844-5

★ **[SIC] by Melissa James Gibson.** In adjacent apartments three young, ambitious neighbors come together to discuss, flirt, argue, share their dreams and plan their futures with unequal degrees of deep hopefulness and abject despair. "A work...concerned with the sound and power of language..." *–NY Times.* "...a wonderfully original take on urban friendship and the comedy of manners—a *Design for Living* for our times..." *–NY Observer.* [3M, 2W] ISBN: 0-8222-1872-0

★ **LOOKING FOR NORMAL by Jane Anderson.** Roy and Irma's twenty-five-year marriage is thrown into turmoil when Roy confesses that he is actually a woman trapped in a man's body, forcing the couple to wrestle with the meaning of their marriage and the delicate dynamics of family. "Jane Anderson's bittersweet transgender domestic comedy-drama ...is thoughtful and touching and full of wit and wisdom. A real audience pleaser." *–Hollywood Reporter.* [5M, 4W] ISBN: 0-8222-1857-7

★ **ENDPAPERS by Thomas McCormack.** The regal Joshua Maynard, the old and ailing head of a mid-sized, family-owned book-publishing house in New York City, must name a successor. One faction in the house backs a smart, "pragmatic" manager, the other faction a smart, "sensitive" editor and both factions fear what the other's man could do to this house— and to them. "If Kaufman and Hart had undertaken a comedy about the publishing business, they might have written *Endpapers*...a breathlessly fast, funny, and thoughtful comedy ...keeps you amused, guessing, and often surprised...profound in its empathy for the paradoxes of human nature." *–NY Magazine.* [7M, 4W] ISBN: 0-8222-1908-5

★ **THE PAVILION by Craig Wright.** By turns poetic and comic, romantic and philosophical, this play asks old lovers to face the consequences of difficult choices made long ago. "The script's greatest strength lies in the genuineness of its feeling." *–Houston Chronicle.* "Wright's perceptive, gently witty writing makes this familiar situation fresh and thoroughly involving." *–Philadelphia Inquirer.* [2M, 1W (flexible casting)] ISBN: 0-8222-1898-4

DRAMATISTS PLAY SERVICE, INC.
440 Park Avenue South, New York, NY 10016 212-683-8960 Fax 212-213-1539
postmaster@dramatists.com   www.dramatists.com